Between Hell and Hope

Teaching Humanity

in an Imperfect World

Leanne Lawrence

For Connie and Leo

DE PROFUNDIS PRODUCTIONS, LLC

ALACHUA, FLORIDA

© 2013

DESIGNED BY CLIFFORD A. SMITH

CSDESIGNSVI.CARBONMADE.COM

FACEBOOK.COM/CSDESIGNSVI

ISBN 978-1-938315-08-4

leanne2blue@gmail.com

FACEBOOK: De Profundis/LeanneLawrence

ON TWITTER: @leanne2blue

WITH DEEPEST GRATITUDE TO: STEVE LAWRENCE, JILL DEUEL, WENDY RICHARDS, HOWARD MINZENBERG, NITA BOONE, THERESA DOWNEY, PIPER REVA, CINDY LEWIS, JENNIFER FORD, AND WILL AND SUZANNE RICHARDSON
• **SPECIAL THANKS TO THE ESPENSHIP FAMILY** •

When Leanne Lawrence decided to take her teaching career to the next level, she had no idea her life would change forever. Immersed in the seedy culture of crime, drugs, prostitution, and violence, her students would challenge her to the very core.

....

"Through very positive insights from her experiences, Leanne opens the reader's eyes to the social issues that have eluded adequate solutions for years. Her work is important to us in continuing to create better outcomes for children in poverty. Thanks to the dedication of persons like herself, some students have been given a better chance....
A very sensitive work."

E. Janet Jamieson, Ed.D: Vermont Social Worker, Teacher and School Superintendent, Ret.

....

"When 60% of students who take the GED exam [in the county jail] pass the test and receive their High School diploma – *this* is the teacher *I* want writing curriculum!"

~Heather Pecora; M.Ed.: Curriculum Specialist
....

"A must-read for anyone who believes we are all connected. 'The Homecoming Queen in the Hood' challenges us all to step up and do what we can to affect change..."

~Wendy Richards: Owner: Noetic Marketing

....

"Leanne Lawrence provides an environment of learning that most of the inmates have never had in their life. Leanne truly cares for her students and pushes them to their highest potential. It's hard to fathom the number of lives that have been touched and changed by this program. It has given confidence to inmates who thought they were not capable of achieving much at all in their lives..."

~Matthew N.: Classroom Tutor

....

"One should only read books which bite and sting.

If the book we are reading does not wake us up with a blow to the head,

what's the point of reading?

A book must be the axe which smashes the frozen sea within us."

~FRANZ KAFKA

TABLE OF CONTENTS

PROLOGUE

It was the fall semester of 2001 and I was teaching a GED class to a group of juvenile boys at the county jail. As the officer escorted the young men into the room, I noticed an extra body. His name wasn't on the list but he'd been in my class before.

"Hello, David," I said smiling as I stood up to hug him.

"Hey, Miss Leanne," he said bowing his head in shame.

"I'm glad you came back to class, sweetie. That took a lot of guts."

"Larry talked me into it, I ain't gonna lie. I was too ashamed."

"Don't you ever be ashamed of trying to create a better life for yourself, David."

"Yeah, I know, Miss Leanne, but the last time I got out I promised you and my mom *and* my grandma that I wouldn't *never* come back to 'dis place!"

"Do you want to talk about it?" "No, ma'am. There ain't no talking to be done.

I guess I'm just *stuck on stupid.*"

We all get 'stuck on stupid,' don't we? We all make mistakes. Being 'Stuck on Stupid' doesn't make us bad people. It doesn't even make us stupid people. It makes us human. Being 'stuck on stupid' only means that we didn't learn our lesson the first time around. The beauty is that we get another chance every single day. I once heard it said: *no matter how far wrong you've gone, you can always turn around.* That's true, isn't it?

As a GED teacher in various settings throughout the community, I work in a world where people have made life-altering mistakes. I strive to give them the tools with which to make different choices, and I work very hard to help them

10

distinguish between what is *easy* and what is *right*. I work with men and women ranging in age from 14 to 70 who challenge me and inspire me on a daily basis and I am grateful for all that I have learned from them.

As you journey through the following pages, I hope to enlighten you and to empower you. More than likely many of these stories will disgust you. I *want* you to be angry. I *want* you to throw this book across the room and yell so loudly that someone will run in and ask what's wrong. I want you to *tell* them what's wrong. I want you to talk about the things that aren't pleasant – the things that aren't discussed at the dinner table or at cocktail parties. I pray we'll all begin to discuss the tragedies of our times.

I believe we have taken political correctness much too far and as a result, we have become numb and apathetic toward one another. The more we ignore this potentially explosive disparity, the farther apart we'll grow. As human beings who share this earth and strive for freedom, tolerance and diversity, we cannot afford to foster the misinterpretation of cultural differences, much less condone it by doing nothing.

Real change in our society, in our neighborhoods, in our schools and in our own homes requires empathy, energy and effort from each and every one of us.

Pencil it in.

INTRODUCTION

"I keep my ideals, because in spite of everything
I still believe that people are really good at heart..."

~Anne Frank

It was a crisp fall day in October of 1978. The sky was an unbelievable blue. As I stood in the middle of my high school football field with my dad by my side, my mind wandered as I stared blankly at the cheering crowd before me...

"In my day, the football players escorted the girls to the field," my dad grumbled the night before. "When did they change it? *Why* did they change it?!" "Calm down, Leo," my mom said rolling her eyes, "you don't have to wear the suit and tie *to* the game, just get changed before half time! God, this is about Leanne, not about you being heckled by your so-called buddies! Relax. I'm sure there'll be plenty of beer left in the cooler when you're done. Pete won't let you die of thirst!"

He wasn't convinced.

The sudden crackling of the microphone jarred me from my trance as Jerry Lockwood, our high school Principal made the much-anticipated announcement. The crowd went wild, and my mom ran onto the field streaming tears of joy. It was there, in the sleepy town of Owego, New York, nestled snugly along the banks of the Susquehanna River, that I was crowned Owego Free Academy's Homecoming Queen.

By the time I realized what had happened and I turned around to hug my dad, he was long gone and headed straight for his tail-gating pals in the parking lot. With his jacket slung over his shoulder, his tie balled up and crammed into his pocket, he was on a mission. Never one to let a friend down, his best buddy Pete met him in the end zone with an ice cold Schlitz. 'Well, that's show biz,' I thought.

Thirty four years later, sans a tiara, my kingdom is the county jail in north central Florida. Here there are no cheering crowds, no roses, no sash, but I do have a title. They call me "The Drive-Thru GED Teacher."

I earned this particular designation by understanding the significance of time as a motivator. The majority of my students have been sentenced to the county jail for a period of three to twelve months with others being shipped off to prison or rehab whenever a bed becomes available. When you don't know how much time you have to work with, it's imperative that you make the most of every minute. If my students – men, women and juveniles – are willing to exert themselves and take advantage of the situation, I can get them from fractions to the Pythagorean Relationship in about a month. Most revel in the opportunity and marvel at the boundlessness of their own abilities. I absolutely love my work and over the course of the last decade I have written about my experiences – some: heartbreaking, others: damn funny, all: life-changing.

You should know that it's taken me more than twelve years to share these stories. Up until this point, writing for me has been cathartic, an often futile attempt to cleanse my mind and my spirit of the ugliness, the sadness and the madness in this world – almost like taking a shower and rinsing away the filth. I have put these words on paper because I need not carry them with me. Once they are in written form, I am free. Make no mistake, not every experience is negative. Oscar Wilde wrote, *"Where there is sorrow - there is holy ground,"* and I thank God for the opportunities afforded me through my job, and I marvel every day at the remarkable tenacity of the human spirit.

It wasn't until my dear friend Wendy Richards, a marketing professional and entrepreneur asked if she could read the stories I had been stuffing into nameless folders for years that the idea of a book became a reality. After reading a few essays she was adamant: "You absolutely *have* to do something with these! They are incredibly powerful and poignant accounts of your life, Leanne! Let's find a way to get them out there and share them with others. These stories could have a huge impact on the lives of many, many people!"

So in 2007, during the Marjorie Kinnan Rawlings Annual Writer's Workshop in Gainesville, FL I invested $100 to spend 30 minutes with a Publishing Agent from New York City. As is customary, I sent her a few of my chapters prior to our appointment so she had something to work with.

The day we met will be one of those stories I'll talk about for a long, long time.

I arrived early and sat in the lobby for a few minutes. When she entered the room and called my name, I got up, smiled, and began walking toward her prepared to shake her hand. Oddly, she looked right past me, scanned the room, and called my name again. When I introduced myself and thanked her for seeing me, she turned pale.

"I'm going to need a few minutes," she said a bit exasperated. "I thought 'Miss. Leanne' was black! Normally I don't enjoy reading anything written in a specific dialect, but you pulled it off – so much so that I thought you were African American!"

She couldn't hustle me into the meeting room quickly enough.

"You do realize this is your hook, don't you?"

"My hook?" I asked, puzzled.

"Your hook is what will grab the reader and pull them in. Your stories are gripping enough, but Leanne, you're not black and you're not a part of this culture. You're an adorable little blonde-haired, blue-eyed, white woman who is completely out of place in this environment. The fact that you're not only accepted by your students, but that you actually make a huge impact is exactly what will make your book sell! Just look at all the crime shows with strong female leads like *Bones, and Law and Order SVU* - and since the majority of readers are women, you'd have an audience who could live vicariously through you. Female detective novels have been best sellers for quite some time; think Patricia Cornwell!"

I was baffled, but determined to get the most out of my investment, "I have a hard time talking about myself," I confessed, "it's not like I'm doing something extraordinary, I just love my work." "Don't you see?" she pushed, "you *are* doing something extraordinary! There aren't very many people who can do what you do and still maintain a positive attitude, let alone still be effective! I would personally be scared to death on a daily basis and could never go into the places you go into with such nonchalance! The best advice I can give you is to make your book panoramic as opposed to episodic. *You* are the story. Weave that concept amongst these powerful essays and that's your book."

So here I am today: *The Homecoming Queen in the Hood.*

Welcome to my world. It's been a remarkable journey, daunting at times, but I'm quite certain I've only just begun. F. Scott Fitzgerald wrote, *"You don't write because you want to say something, you write because you've got something to say."* Well, my friends, I've got something to say.

The following pages will take you from the classroom to the courtroom to the county jail. This is who I am. My message is simple:

Do What You Can.

Speak Your Truth.

May you find meaning in these words, and purpose in your heart.

GOT THEM GROCERY AISLE BLUES

Got Them Grocery Aisle Blues

I'm hungry, I'm tired – ain't got nothin' to lose.

Cigarettes and beer – I can't see clear – won't show no fear…

I'm hungry, I'm tired, I'm screamin' out loud - I'm dragged
past the Pop Tarts through the blank-faced crowd.

Got Them Grocery Aisle Blues

Wearin' my big brother's shoes – my mom's all outta booze –
if I had to choose,

I'd be any place but here.

It don't seem fair – people just stare – They don't say nothin' at
all,

Just turn their heads when I fall – ain't got no one to call…

Got Them Grocery Aisle Blues

My dad's out of jail – my mom's lookin' pale. Gotta move on,
gotta leave in the night-

Gotta run to some town before he guns us all down.

Don't know what we will eat – don't know where we will sleep
- It don't matter to me – I'll **never** be free…

Got Them Grocery Aisle Blues

My sister's knocked up – my ma's boyfriend's the dad – Means he wasn't on me.

Life ain't so bad. She's only thirteen, tried to stay clean – But livin' like this makes you bitter and mean.

Got Them Grocery Aisle Blues

The heat got shut off, I'm freezin' my ass. My teacher keeps askin' why I don't come to class. My clothes are too small, I ain't got no coat – rich kids suck, I don't give a fuck!

Can't pay the bills, I got the chills. Wish I could eat. Back out on the street – nothin' here but hate – it don't fill your plate.

Mom's passed out on the bathroom floor.

Call 9-11 and throw the goddamn needle out the fuckin' back door.

Got Them Grocery Aisle Blues

The screamin' won't stop – the neighbors are pissed.

Nobody should have to live like this.

She got punched in the face – there's blood on the floor, there's blood on his hands – can't take it no more – wish my mind could erase the shame that I feel.

No one to tell, no one will hear.

I just wanna yell…this must be hell…

Ain't there nobody out there?

I wrote this poem in five minutes. I had just moved to central Florida and had been swimming at the lake all day with my three old dogs. It was a long and beautiful day with friends and I was ready to relax, but before I could sit down, the words, "Got Them Grocery Aisle Blues" popped into my head and I had to write them down. Within minutes, the rest of the words spilled from my mind faster than I could get them on paper. I shoved the scribbled poem into a kitchen drawer and went about my day.

A few weeks later, I saw an advertisement for poets and writers to submit their work to the *25th Annual Mount Dora Spring Festival: A Celebration of Music & Literature.* I dug the crumpled piece of paper out of the drawer, typed it up and with tongue in cheek, mailed it in. 'Let's just see how *celebratory* the people of Mount Dora really are.'

About a month later, I received a letter with the *Mt. Dora Spring Festival* logo in the corner. Quite certain it would read something like: *'Thank you for your submission, please don't ever set foot in Mt. Dora as long as you live.'* I was prepared. Much to my surprise, it read, *'Congratulations! You have been awarded first place in the Mount Dora Spring Festival Writer's Contest for your entry of a poem entitled, GOT THEM GROCERY AISLE BLUES.'* They even shared with me some of the judges' comments: *"Powerful image and presentation; not your grandmother's poetry, theme, language and structure form a powerful reflection of modern life,"* etc.

The poem was printed in its entirety in a couple of local newspapers and I was asked to attend the reception and read the poem aloud to an audience at the Mt. Dora Center for the Arts. Read it aloud? 'Wait a minute,' I thought. 'This poem has two fucks and a goddamn in it; are people ready for this?'

Ready they were. The reaction that evening from those in attendance would change my life. In fact, it would be the catalyst for all of my future writing. These people were honest and open about their own personal experiences, and many waited in line for over an hour just to get a chance to talk to me.

Some asked if the poem was autobiographical, perhaps because they sought solidarity, or because they could relate to the sadness and just wanted to be heard.

By far the most beautiful experience of the day was watching people - total strangers, comfort one another while waiting in line and long after the reception had ended. Amazing, I thought. There is so much pain in this world, but as history has proven time and time again, we need each other.

So here's to the judges and the staff in Mount Dora. Your brave and open-minded stance may have sparked a revolution. Cheers.

> *"Childhood is the kingdom where nobody dies…"*
>
> ~Edna St. Vincent Millay

Imagine if you will, a frail and frightened little girl curled up in a ball crying and praying and trying to stay quiet because HE said if she doesn't shut up, HE'LL kill her. She is soaked with sweat and blood, and terror has caused her to saturate her clothes with urine. Her mind races and she asks herself, "*Why didn't you just clean up your room, you knew it would make HIM mad if HE came home and it wasn't clean. Why do you always do things that upset HIM? You really are a pain in the ass and you deserve everything you get!*"

Seconds later, the closet door bursts open and she is snatched from her pathetic hiding place with massive force, snared by stumpy, hairy fingers that wrap around her little arm like the talons of a hawk seizing an unsuspecting creature from the earth.

Imagine the thoughts racing around in her little brain: "*Will I die today? If God really loved me, why would he allow*

HIM to do this to me? Will I ever see my mom and my baby brother again? Will HE hurt them, too? If only I had cleaned my room…"

Imagine the pain she feels from the vice-like grip clamped on to her tiny arm.

Imagine a broken woman cowering in the corner forced to witness the brutal assault. Imagine the helplessness in her mother's eyes, the wrenching pain she feels for her innocent baby girl. Imagine the black eyes on the mother's face, the broken ribs that have not yet healed from the last raid on her battered, weary body. Imagine the dark circles under those eyes from night after endless night of enduring the pain and wrath of HIS insecurities.

Imagine the little girl flying through the air, her blood and urine-soaked nightgown clinging to her sweaty little frame. Imagine a pain so intense that it numbs her entire body as she is slammed against the kitchen wall. *"If only I had cleaned my room…"* She cringes as the MONSTER returns. HE is drooling and laughing and shouting as HE seizes her limp little body and screams that this is *"ALL HER FAULT!"*

The veins pop out of HIS neck and forehead, throbbing and glaring at her, reaching out for her like tentacles. HE turns and slowly licks HIS lips to taunt the mother who is pleading and quivering and powerless to put an end to the fury. The iron-fisted DEMON cackles and seizes the fallen angel, dragging her from under the kitchen chair. HIS huge chest heaves in and out and the all-too-familiar smell of sweat and beer permeate the room. HE grins like an evil clown. HIS yellow, horse-like teeth take phantom bites at the air. HIS fierce glare pierces the air like a switchblade slicing through flesh: *"I'M the fucking BOSS of this house and don't you ever forget it!"*

HE howls at the helpless mother as HE mocks the little girl's cries. Terrified, exhausted and deflated, she hangs her head in shame and another piece of her silently dies.

Imagine the sound of her baby's body breaking as HE hurls her once again toward the wall like a major league pitcher aiming for the glove. Imagine the terror and the anticipation, the blood dripping, the tears flowing. Imagine the sound of silence broken only by the sound of a tiny voice begging for mercy…

Now. Imagine she's *yours.*

.~.~.~.~.~.~.~.~.~

On a global scale, we face an epidemic of abuse in many, many forms. Women, children, immigrants, minorities, the elderly, the disabled, and animals – all face unthinkable cruelty and death on a daily basis. Why? Because evil wears many disguises and manifests itself in countless forms.

It's not always the man in the trench coat hiding in the bushes; evil lurks within the souls of our husbands and our wives, our fathers and our mothers, our aunts and our uncles, our granddads and our grandmas. Evil disguises itself as priests, clergy, coaches, and community leaders, health-care providers, daycare workers, and seemingly normal, everyday, honest-to-goodness, ordinary people. Every family has skeletons, but that which turns some of us into monsters lies deep in the abyss of our childhoods and in our psyches. I will never attempt to understand it nor explain it, but *it* is out there and it's up to us to speak for those who cannot speak for themselves.

If *you* are being battered, please know that you are beautiful and intelligent and creative and capable. **Please know that you deserve better**. There *is* a way out, believe me. There *are* people out there who care and there are dozens of resources to help you and your loved ones find freedom. In the back of this book you will find an Appendix with vital hotline numbers and websites listing organizations that exist solely to help you get out safely and live the life you deserve. May it be your guide and may it set you free.

Change is up to us, my friends. Each and every one of you reading this book has picked it up for a reason. It was no accident that it landed in your hands. Each of you has the true capacity to affect change. I challenge you all to step up and do what you can to stop the madness. Stop supporting abuse in any and every form. If you know someone who is battering their spouse or abusing their children or even their animals – *make the call.* You can remain anonymous and you will have done something extraordinary. Saving a life is no small feat.

The Early Years

It was 1983 and, after graduating from Jacksonville University in Florida, I returned home to teach at my old high school. My grandfather was gravely ill at the time, and I wanted to be close. He died in October of 1983 and I was by his bedside when he took his last breath. I wouldn't have wanted to be anywhere else.

My first year out of the gate was spent as a Resource Room teacher at my old high school where I assisted students with special needs by helping with homework, creating workable schedules and providing moral support. My room fast became the safe haven and a cool place to hang out – contrary to the stigma usually attached to this type of setting. It was an awesome year and a perfect way to get my feet wet. Since I had only graduated four years prior, it was a little odd going from student to colleague, but the faculty was incredibly supportive and made my inaugural encounter relatively smooth and uneventful.

The following fall, I was offered a job at an elementary school in the same district as the Special Education teacher for a group of five to twelve-year-olds with varying levels of disability.

I can only describe the following two years as "Mr. Toad's Wild Ride."

Buckle up.

> *"When I dare to be powerful,*
> *to use my strength in the service of my vision,*
> *then it becomes less and less important whether I am afraid..."*
>
> ~Audre Lord

They said she had been so badly abused as an infant that she would never function 'normally' in society.

They said the memories of her early years would haunt her for the rest of her life.

They said the details of her childhood would make you sick.

They said, "If you read her file, you will have nightmares and you will be forever changed."

They were right.

When I met MaryAgnes, she was seven years old. She was unpredictable and angry. She was rude and controlling, and like a feral child, she devoured those around her. She had recently been adopted by a local couple – both in their mid-forties and both professionals. It was my second year of teaching and I was still working under 'probationary' conditions. After three years of satisfactory performance, a teacher is granted 'tenure,' and his or her job is secure.

I had been assigned to a self-contained Special Education classroom at a local elementary school. This was long before the concept of "mainstreaming" had hit the mainstream. "Self-contained" simply meant that my students would be with me the majority of the day and they would leave the room for Art, Music, and Gym, but they weren't scheduled to 'blend in' with other students. I was responsible for the education and socialization of ten students ranging in age from five to twelve. Each beautiful little person had his or her own distinct personality. Two of my boys, both five, had Down's Syndrome; another, also five, had been born with Fetal Alcohol Syndrome. His mother drank heavily during her pregnancy and he became an alcoholic in the womb (similar to crack babies). Another five- year-old was doing his best to stay ambulatory, but was fighting a losing battle to Muscular Dystrophy. The oldest boy, age nine, was suspected of setting the fire that destroyed his parent's home; apparently he was sick and tired of his father molesting his older sister.

The others were plunked in my room because no one else wanted to deal with them and I was the proverbial 'new kid on the block.' Sure, some had minor learning disabilities, but most were considered to have behavior problems and could not be allowed to upset the old apple cart in a regular classroom. I learned quickly about the practice of dumping the 'unwanted' and 'unruly' children into a Special Ed. Classroom.

As was customary, I paid a quick visit to my new room over the summer and was greeted by the outgoing teacher. I had known her since high school and she hadn't changed a bit. She was sweet and pretty, and perhaps a little more perky than any one person should be, but some people are just born that way. She shared with me her behavior management system, and graciously offered to provide any assistance she could before she moved away.

Neat pieces of poster board with the name of each student in bright colors hung on the wall near her desk. Shining stars and colorful stickers indicated who had been a "good listener" or a "good helper" that day. She was a born teacher and the kids loved her. Once I had gotten the essence of how things worked, I wished her well and headed for the door when she chirped, "Oh, Leanne, one more thing. This is for MaryAgnes."

From her neatly organized bottom drawer, Little Miss Sunshine produced what she called a "disciplinary tool." MaryAgnes' adoptive parents had provided for her to use in the classroom. I must have looked absolutely horrified, because she immediately placed a kind hand on my shoulder and said, "Oh, don't worry sweetie, it's just like the one they use at home."

I felt nauseous.

"Believe me," she continued with a wink, "MaryAgnes hates it – most of the time all I have to do is open that bottom drawer and she straightens right up. Unfortunately, there have been a few times when I've had to use it."

"I don't understand," I said feeling suddenly wounded. "They expect me to use a paddle on a child who has been severely abused and tortured for the majority of her short life?"

"Well, yeah. You see, Leanne, her parents want the discipline to be consistent with the Behavior Management Program they use at home."

I felt hot and my knees were about to betray me. "Let me get this straight," I whimpered. "She was 'rescued' from the horrors of her childhood by her adoptive parents."

She nodded innocently.

"Both of whom are well-educated professionals."

"Uh huh," she agreed.

I took a deep breath and looked straight into her beautiful eyes. "I wouldn't use a paddle on an animal."

I picked up the doodad like it was radioactive and hurled it into the big gray metal trash can. The sound pounded in my head and echoed like a giant drum. I clearly remember holding the paddle in my hand and even for that split second, it felt slimy and rotten and perverse. She looked at me sympathetically and shook her head saying, "It's my understanding that this is only your second year in this district, Leanne. You'll never get your tenure if you buck these people, you know that."

I was doing my best not to judge my colleague because I knew in my heart she was a very sweet person and an excellent teacher. I also knew she was right. They were influential people and I'm sure she felt trapped. As I tried hard to contain my anger and disgust, I asked a simple question, already knowing the answer, "Does the Principal know about this?" "No," she answered, avoiding eye contact and looking to the floor for the first time. "MaryAgnes' parents said that since I wouldn't actually be using it that much, because, like I said, just the sight of it scares her to death, well, they didn't think anyone else needed to know."

I felt truly sad for her. Sad that they had threatened her with her job and had more than likely made her life a living hell. "I'm sorry they got to you," I said sincerely, and walked out of the room. This would not be the last time I stepped into the ring with MaryAgnes' parents; I had no idea however, that the next bout would rival Frasier and Ali.

MaryAgnes was extremely low-functioning. She was easily distracted and highly emotional. Her own survival instincts ruled the limited sphere in which she lived and breathed and she tried desperately to control everything and everyone around her. Her outbursts were violent at first, but when put to the test, a warm hug and a little alone time with me or my assistant were pretty effective deterrents to erratic and harmful behavior.

I did my best to respect her parent's wishes and work on academic skills they deemed appropriate, but we were on opposite sides of the fence when it came to her ability level. As a matter of fact, my goal for that year was to make her feel safe and loved, and to give her plenty of room to explore this strange world without feeling threatened. Of course we worked on reading, math and language skills, and she was innately intelligent and eager to learn.

One fall afternoon, I received a phone call from her dad, an executive with a big chair, a big office, and a super-sized ego: "Leanne, you *are* aware of the fact that MaryAgnes can read, aren't you?"I suddenly remember feeling bad for him. This child could *not* read, but we were making strides and she was enjoying each new experience. Nevertheless, her parents believed it was necessary to call me on the carpet for "wasting their time," and "hindering her progress."

I had to assume they were still pretty irked for the humiliation they suffered at the hands of my Principal when he found out about the 'disciplinary tool.' So the father asked me to come to his office for a face-to-face chat. As I sat there like a child who had been sent to the Principal's office, I remember him saying something like, "Leanne, I know you're new, but our daughter is much more advanced than you're giving her credit for. And this busy work you're sending home is much too easy … blahblahblahblahblah." (Close your eyes and imagine the nasal drone of the faceless teacher in the Charlie Brown specials.) "We need you to work with us, not against us."

"But, Mr. Smith," I said objectively, "based on my observation, MaryAgnes really can't read."

"You see, Leanne," he said in that condescending tone that made me want to spit, "you can ask our friends. MaryAgnes loves reading out loud when we have company. Honestly, people can't believe how far she's come," he said with a wink and an arrogant smirk.

'Oh, great' I thought, ' a circus side-show act.'

As MaryAgnes grew ever more lovable and capable in the classroom, as well as in Gym class, Music, and Art, the other teachers applauded her progress, and her parents grew ever more impatient with me and my teaching style.

"We've tried working with you, Leanne, but we're just going to have to go over your head." As was typical, they conveniently by-passed my boss and went directly to the big cheese, the Director of Education. I imagined their plea: "Look, Dr. Boone, we realize Leanne is a new teacher, but we can no longer stand by and allow her to waste our daughter's precious time. We've worked too hard and come too far to stand by and watch this happen."

Dr. Boone had no choice but to call me in. "Close the door, kid," he said shaking his head. "Now what the hell is going on?"

I explained my side of the story and backed everything up with proof – daily academic exercises that documented her level of functioning. I sort of felt sorry for him. It was painfully obvious that he dreaded the thought of facing them again. He was a true professional and I had nothing but sincere respect for him, but I wasn't about to budge on this one. And, true to form, he didn't ask me to, but before he could attempt to speak to them on my behalf, however, MaryAgnes' parents had already requested that the School Board hold a special session where they would ask the board members to demand my apology or accept my resignation, whichever came first. Thankfully, Dr. Boone was able to convince them that a full-blown School Board meeting was not necessary at that time, but that he would present all pertinent information to the members at the next meeting.

They agreed to a more intimate gathering that included Dr. Boone, the school Principal, and me. Due, however, to a history of irreconcilable differences between my boss and MaryAgnes' dad, the Principal was only allowed to attend the meeting if he agreed to have no verbal input whatsoever. 'Great, I'm dead.'

D-Day arrived and our school secretary buzzed me on my classroom wall phone: "You ready for this, kid?" she asked with a chuckle.

I could picture her shaking her head, and in her tone I sensed a fusion of sympathy and utter disgust. She knew as well as anyone how ridiculous this whole thing was and how far MaryAgnes had come. I believe she would've gone into battle with me if she could have.

So I left my kids with my teacher's assistant and began the seemingly endless journey down the long hallway to a cramped meeting room where I would more than likely crash and burn. I remember trying to cheer myself up by thinking, "Hey, a career change isn't such a bad idea. Will that be paper or plastic, ma'am?" Ha Ha.

I walked into the room and there they were, perched smugly next to Dr. Boone. The proud parents and their child prodigy had come prepared. In fact, they were loaded for bear. On the other side of the table sat my loyal boss. He had been made aware of the ground rules and was obviously not pleased. He looked me in the eyes helplessly and apologetically. I just shrugged and whispered "Thanks for being here."

Before Dr. Boone had a chance to set the agenda, 'dad' snatched a naughahide brief case from under his chair and plunked on the table with a loud thud. Then slowly and deliberately he undid the latch. The ringmasters brought with them a secret weapon, an arsenal of doom, if you will. As 'mom' held it gingerly in her hands, almost caressing it, like one of the women on The Price is Right, we saw that it was a book – an innocent children's book with which they had hoped to seal my fate. Then, with all the pomp and circumstance of a presidential inauguration, they prepared their audience for a bona fide miracle: "MaryAgnes, read this book," they commanded.

And read it she did, word for word. She read the book perfectly and without error. It was really quite impressive. As she stood there proudly grinning from ear to ear, she waited anxiously for her reward – the rest of us waited for them to throw her a biscuit or pat her on the head. Bravo! They were almost in tears, they were so proud. Turning self-importantly to the Director they said, "See, we told you Leanne was wasting our time. Now what are you going to do about it?" My boss nearly leapt from his seat and Dr. Boone motioned for him to calm down. He looked at me with sympathy and concern: "Leanne?" he almost pleaded.

I remember feeling like a death row inmate who had just been granted a last-minute pardon. *Could it really be this simple?* Strategically positioned in the corner of the room was an easel with a big blank piece of white paper clipped to the top. A black Sharpie marker rested in the tray. I had asked the school secretary to put them there that morning.

"Hi sweetie," I said to MaryAgnes as I stood and headed slowly for the easel. She was happy to have me in the room, and predictably, she jumped up, ran over and hugged me hard. You could have cut the tension with a knife. I was actually hoping they didn't bring one of those too! "Can I take a look at your favorite book, honey?" She beamed and offered it to me with glee and said, "I can read Ms. Lawrence. My mom and dad are very happy with me!" "I know you can, honey," I said with tears welling up in my eyes. "You were great!"

As I purposefully skimmed over the simple prose, I knew that in my hands I held the deed to my future. Moving casually and deliberately, I picked up the black marker and began to write on the huge piece of blank paper. I looked up innocently and caught their eyes – they appeared to be ill, seasick almost. My boss looked like he had just won the lottery, and the color seemed to seep back into Dr. Boone's face within a matter of seconds. I had chosen a simple word from the book. I had taken it out of context, out of the realm of memorization, and wrote it on the blank page, nice and big.

"Can you tell me what this word is, sweetie?"

As you may have guessed, MaryAgnes had absolutely no idea what I had written on the paper. Bless her heart. She had memorized the book, word-for-word. It's called 'rote' learning, a simple survival mechanism she had learned and perfected.

I almost felt bad for them. Their heads were bowed and they looked deflated. Victory was mine, but it was bittersweet, and I didn't feel at all like gloating.

> *"We find delight in the beauty and happiness of children
> that makes the heart too big for the body..."*
>
> ~Emerson

He was Joie De Vivre in a 40-pound frame.

He was like a fly that couldn't light in one spot for more than a *nano*second at a time.

He was scrawny, and like a stick figure, his head was too big for his body.

He spoke in a language all his own.

He was five and coming to school for the first time.

He drank coffee for breakfast.

He was Raymond Charles Davis.

Diagnosis: Fetal Alcohol Syndrome.

These children are born addicted to alcohol. Most are developmentally delayed and have severe learning disabilities. His mother was young, without hope and drank heavily during her pregnancy. When the doctors told her that her child would be born mentally retarded, it was more than she could bear. So she made the painstaking decision to put him up for adoption. Her aging parents, who had already raised six children of their own, would not hear of it. Although Mrs. Davis, a warm, caring and loving woman with a quick wit and easy smile, was totally blind, she and her husband brought the baby home and raised him as their own. He would call them 'Ma' and 'Pa.'

He hated food. He loved the playground. He lived to swing.

On the first day of school, as we took our places in the cafeteria, the rest of the class was in awe of the experience. Sounds of lunchroom chatter filled the air, the lunch ladies told them how big they were and the older kids waved. As they shared their lunch together as a group, each little cherub sat up straight and proud. Everyone, that is, except Raymond. He was absolutely miserable as he sat there staring pitifully at the naked hot dog the lunch lady had stuffed in a bun and plopped on his tray.

"Why don't you put some ketchup on it Ray?" I asked innocently.

"Oh, God no lady, I hate ketchup. Makes me sick. Can we go swing now?"

"Not until you eat your lunch, Raymond. Come on, it looks pretty good to me; why don't you dig into that delicious applesauce?"

"Ick, lady, pwea (please), can't we go outside now?" He was pale.

"Raymond, Ma told me that you love hot dogs and applesauce. Besides, everyone else is almost finished eating. I guess I'll just have to stay in here with you while the other kids go out on the playground and swing."

Panic set in. The thought of missing out on the playground compelled him to act. Frantic, he grabbed the bun and squeezed it so hard the hot dog shot out and flew across the room like an ballistic missile. The shriveled piece of meat landed on the floor like a lead balloon and rolled silently under the table. By this time, the rest of the kids were howling, but not Ray. He was on a mission. He jumped up from his seat, danced around a little like he had to pee, and crawled under the table. When he emerged, he held the hot dog high above his head like a golfer who had successfully retrieved his best ball from the drink. The crowd went wild! He gave it a quick once-over and shouted, "No hair on it!" and then sunk his teeth into the end like a Viking at a victory feast.

His delightful little face suddenly turned pitiful and distorted. He looked like he'd just bitten the head off a live lizard. I was doing all I could not to crack up. I felt really awful, but Ma and Pa had asked that I make him at least try his lunch, so I hung tough.

"Good job, Ray. That wasn't so bad, was it? Now why don't you try a little of that corn?" With a pathetic grimace, he chewed the microscopic piece of hot dog as if he was eating raw sewage and swallowed with a loud and dramatic gulp. Then he picked up a teeny kernel of corn and placed it hesitantly on his tongue. His mouth was wide open and the little yellow kernel just sat there like a throat lozenge waiting to do its job. His eyes were shut and his expression was one of sheer terror, petrified that he might actually swallow it. "Go ahead, Ray, chew that up so we can go swing!"

He was in hell.

I couldn't take any more, so I decided to give him a break and mingle with the rest of the class. I looked up and down the lunch table at the perfect little faces that were my new students and all was right in the world. It was only my second year in the district and I would fall in love with these children.

Lunchtime was over and we were ready to line up and head back to our room. I glanced nonchalantly at Raymond's tray and it was suspiciously bare. Distressed, he looked up at me and yelled loudly, "Lady, I all done – peel my pate!"

"Wow, Ray, you finished most of your lunch – good for you, buddy!"

"*Peel my pate!*" he demanded.

"Well, I don't have to *feel your plate*, honey; I can see that it's empty. I am really proud of you, Raymond. Wait until I tell Ma and Pa what a big boy you were in the lunch room!" (Remember that Ma is blind, and the only way she could tell if he had finished his meal was to *feel his plate)*. Just as he was about to jump up and head for the door, I feigned innocence and asked, "Uh, what's that you've got under the table there, Ray?"

His eyes began to shift from side to side like a Russian spy in an old black and white foreign film. His jaw dropped and he sat there perfectly still with his mouth wide open and gaping. He looked like a mounted fish. For a split second, I wasn't sure if he was going to make a run for it or simply faint and fall right out of his chair. He was desperately seeking an answer, looking around the room like a game show contestant scanning the audience for a clue. When he realized the cavalry wasn't coming, he looked up at me innocently and muttered, "Nutting."

"Nothing? Okay. Then let's line up and head out." I was trying to give him a break, but he was frozen solid. In a valiant attempt to be helpful, Stevie, a beautiful little five-year-old with Muscular Dystrophy, bent over and peeked under the table. He straightened up really fast "Eeeeewwwww, Miss Lawrence, there's chunks of something gross dripping right through his fingers!"

Stevie was a mossy shade of green – uh oh! I was praying he wouldn't throw up. I could handle spit, blood and broken bones, but barf? No way. If he had hurled on the floor, it would have been an all-out barf-o-rama! "Raymond? Talk to me, buddy!" I said as I tried to maintain my composure. His big brown eyes were still searching the room. Slowly he pulled his hands out from under the table and revealed the clandestine truth. Gobs of apple sauce oozed through the tiny fingers of his left hand, and chunks of mushy yellow corn from the fingers of his right. He looked like a deflated balloon. I smiled softly and shook my head: "You'd better plop that stuff back on your tray and wash those hands, buddy. You earned yourself a sticker for being honest today, Ray!"

The color began to seep back into his face; he had been delivered! The other 75 students in the cafeteria broke into thunderous applause and Ray began dancing around the room like Muhammed Ali. There he stood at the cafeteria entrance, all 40 pounds of him, waving and beaming and reveling in his new-found fame. Even the lunch ladies gave him a standing ovation. Then suddenly, he jumped up on a metal folding chair and held his hands high above his head, waving the peace sign. Now he looked like Richard Nixon standing in front of the cameras assuring the nation he was "not a crook." It was on that cool fall day when the air was crisp and the leaves were turning crimson, that Raymond Charles Davis was declared the 'Mayor' of Apalachin Elementary School.

Each new day would begin the same. Stick-figure Raymond would flit into the classroom leaving his belongings strewn down the hallway like bread crumbs in a dense forest left behind to ensure his safe return home.

"Goo-monin' Me Wonant!" he would shout gleefully as he tumbled with reckless abandon into my classroom each morning. "Haddy Birdy!" Translation: "Good Morning, Ms. Lawrence! Happy Birthday!"

"Good morning, Raymond," I would reply with a smirk, "but today's not my birthday. Thank you just the same."

The only food Raymond would eat without gagging was birthday cake. I think he truly believed he could manifest the celebratory confection just by wishing me "Happy Birthday" on a daily basis.

"What did you have for breakfast this morning, Ray?"

"A cud-o-coddee," (a cup of coffee) he would exclaim matter-of-factly as he fluttered about the room on his tiptoes touching everything in sight, humming his favorite tune ("You Are My Sunshine") and greeting each of the other kids with a gentle pat on the head.

"Ray, I thought I told you to tell Ma that you couldn't have coffee for breakfast anymore," I said smiling and shaking my head, anticipating his response.

"Oh, don't worry, Me Wonant, it was de-caddinated," (Oh, don't worry, Ms. Lawrence, it was decaffeinated)!

The rest of the kids would crack up and roll their eyes because by this time, young Raymond had already started a puzzle and left it unfinished all over the floor, made a couple of scribbles on a piece of drawing paper calling it homework, and summoned the main office from the wall phone. When he had finished his 'conversation,' he would simply drop the receiver and the phone would dangle helplessly from its cord and bounce off the wall like a rock climber with a busted cable. I would hear Mrs. Gee, our awesome school secretary, laughing on the other end. It was the morning ritual.

As the year progressed and I grew closer to my students, I began to role play. It's a wonderful teaching tool and is particularly helpful with abused children (as you'll read elsewhere in a much less amusing chapter of this book). If Ray was involved, however, role playing was always an adventure.

One afternoon, my teacher's assistant and dear friend, Charlene Iacovazzi (pronounced Yah-co-vazzi) and I were sitting on the floor with the class when Ray jumped up to put a book back on the shelf. Not paying attention, he accidentally hit Charlene in the head with it. Without missing a beat, Iacovazzi, one of the funniest people I've ever met, slumped over and pretended she had been knocked out. She caught us all totally off guard, but not Raymond – he took action! Before I knew what was happening, he had grabbed the wall phone and was yelling, "MAYDAY, MAYDAY, MIDDA GEE, MIDDA GEE – HELP HELP, WADOBAZZI HAD A HEART ATTACK!!! CALL THE WAMBULANCE, CALL THE SQUAD, WADOBAZZI'S DOWN!!! Translation: "Mayday, Mrs. Gee Iacovazzi had a heart attack … call the emergency squad … Iacovazzi's down!"

Ray dropped the phone and left it dangling as he always did, and ran out of the room. From what I could gather, he was flitting down the hallway of the Primary Wing, jumping up and down and knocking on every door yelling, "HELP, HELP, WADOBAZZI'S DOWN!! COME QUICK!WADOBAZZI HAD A HEART ATTACK!"

Then as Charlene and I watched helplessly, he ran past our room, skipping really, headed straight for the school nurse."HELP, HELP, MIDDA JONNA (Mrs. Johnson), WADOBAZZI NEEDS CPR! CALL THE SQUAD." (Emergency Squad.)

It pains me to admit this, but there was absolutely nothing I could do. Charlene and I, along with the rest of the class, were laughing so hard we couldn't do much of anything. Mrs. Gee and Mrs. Johnson, and *every* teacher in our wing (6 or 7 of them) abandoned their students and their duties and rushed to my room only to find the two adults responsible for this debacle rolling helplessly on the floor. Tears were running down our cheeks and all we could do was shrug our shoulders and whimper a feeble apology over the 'slight misunderstanding.'

As the new kid on the block, I would pay for this one for a *long* time. Thanks, 'Wadobazzi,' you're the best!

The end of the year was fast approaching and for some unknown reason, the rookie teacher hadn't had enough ribbing from the elders in the building, so I decided to put on a Christmas Play. Since I had seven boys and two girls, I thought it would be amusing if I re-wrote "Snow White and the Seven Dwarfs." I'd call it "Snow Bound and the Seven Drifts."

The kids were thrilled. I think they were actually more excited that Charlene would be playing the wicked witch, so every afternoon we practiced, and we practiced, and we practiced some more. Unfortunately, and somewhat suspiciously I might add, the night before the big event, poor Charlene called me at home to tell me she was sick. She felt awful about it, but said she couldn't get out of bed. I was desperate so I called Michele a dear friend of mine who was already a crucial part of the plan. As a master seamstress she made all of our costumes. She even designed the green felt, curly-toed shoes for the seven drifts. I begged her to stand in for Charlene because without the evil step-mother, there was no play! Michele used to sing in a band and I didn't think she'd suffer stage fright. Without hesitation, she agreed and yes, the show would go on. No offense, Michele, you were an awesome witch!

Mr. Orlando, our school Principal, was extremely supportive and decided to make a big deal out of this particular event. The day before the curtain rose, he came into my room and gathered my kids together in a semi-circle like troops preparing for battle. He told them if they were really good and remembered their lines, he had a big surprise for them when the play was over. He told them he had cake! Why didn't I think of that?

So the following morning Mr. Orlando took center stage in the school auditorium in front of a standing-room-only crowd and proudly stated, "Ladies and Gentlemen, please give a warm welcome to Ms. Lawrence's class as they perform "Snow Bound and the Seven Drifts!"

The room broke into thunderous applause and my kids beamed. Bless you, Frank Orlando. I know you and my mom had your moments, but in my eyes, you were one hell of a boss.

Earlier that week, the class had taken a vote and decided Raymond would be the emcee. God help us. Ray was also cast as 'Drifty,' Dopey's illegitimate brother. Don't ask. I had the backstage jitters, and thought I'd better check on Raymond to make sure he hadn't come down with a sudden case of stage fright. Not the 'Mayor.' He was cool as a cucumber and he looked absolutely adorable. Ma and Pa had taken him to J.J. Newberry's Five and Ten Cent Store and bought him a new pair of navy blue polyester slacks with a permanent, sewn-in crease. To complete the ensemble, they picked out a short-

sleeved checkered dress shirt and a matching blue clip-on tie.
They put a little, (well, a lot) of 'Dippity-Doo' in his hair,
parted it on one side and slicked it down real good. I could
hardly stand it; he stood there so straight and proud with his
scrawny little arms poking out of his new shirt like stick arms
on a snowman, and he danced around back stage like he had to
pee.

"DO you have to pee, Raymond?" I asked nervously.

"Nope," he replied with confidence. "Don't worry, Me
Wonant, I won't pee my pants!" I found no comfort.

The curtain rose and the 'Mayor' strode onto the stage
with more savvy than Bob Barker himself. He went straight to
his mark in front of the microphone perched on its stand. So
far, so good. Everyone was holding their breath and when he
took his *first* bow, the crowd went wild. I was standing in the
pit in front of the stage looking up at him and giving him a
'thumbs up.' Before I could give him his first cue, Raymond
began sashaying across the stage from left to right, bowing non-

stop like the Austrian woman at the end of the talent contest in *The Sound of Music*. Realizing we hadn't even gotten through the introduction, I tapped the floor with my clipboard in a futile attempt to bring him back down to earth. O.K., perhaps I did more than 'tap' the floor, I don't remember really. Maybe I actually 'banged' the stage with a little more force than I realized, but the interaction had the whole auditorium in stitches and Ray hadn't even opened his mouth!

He finally stopped bowing and looked at me for a signal. "Thank you, Jesus," I thought, and nodded for him to begin.

"Wadies and Gennemen!" he roared. "Welcome to my pway! Thank you, Me Wonant!"

Now it was my turn. I had made huge signs from bright yellow poster board and laminated them to assist the audience with 'Ray-speak.' I held them high like a protester at a rally:

The first sign went up and said: *Translation*

Then came sign number 2:   *Ladies and Gentlemen,*

| Number 3: | *Welcome to our play!* |
| And number 4: | *Thank you! (he wasn't* |

supposed to thank ME!)

| Cue: | Bow and leave stage. |

The crowd leapt to their feet. Man, was he a natural. He bowed some more and smiled that sweet Raymond smile and motioned for everyone to take their seats. 'Way to go, Ray,' I thought. 'Maybe we'll get through this after all.'

No such luck. Just when I thought I hadn't made the biggest career faux pas of my life, he snatched the microphone from the stand, snaked the cord around with his other hand like some cheesy lounge singer, strode to the middle of the stage and like Jesse Jackson at a campaign rally, began working the crowd.

"Wadies and Gennemen, Hewo there evybody! My name is Raymond Charles Davis. Now sit down and be kyet (quiet) and we'll all have some cake!"

I tapped (alright, banged) the floor again but 'Mr. Entertainment' had the crowd in the palm of his hand. Visions of Englebert Humperdink gyrating on some Las Vegas stage suddenly flashed before my eyes and I felt woozy. Doing my best to remain calm, I half-whispered/half-yelled from the pit "cut it out, NOW, Raymond and give me back that mike!"

Looking down at me from the middle of the stage, he pointed his bony little finger at me and directly into the microphone, he whispered the unthinkable: *"Not now, Me Wonant!"* (Not now, Ms. Lawrence!) The room was alive with laughter and Raymond Charles Davis was in heaven.

Then suddenly, as if taken over by an out-of-body experience, he closed his eyes and broke out into the chorus of his favorite song, *You Are My Sunshine.* The only words he really knew and could *kind* of pronounce were *"shine, shine, shine…"* but he sang them with more passion than Pavarotti himself and brought down the house.

"The show must go on," I groaned, so I grabbed the cord and began reeling him in like the catch of the day. He held on tight right to the end. In fact, we were eyeball to eyeball by the time he reached the end of his rope, so to speak. With a loud and deliberate gulp, he dramatically loosened his clip-on tie, sneaked back to the center of the stage and took a final bow. *I*, on the other hand, took six aspirin with a Diet Coke and prayed aloud for the final curtain.

We performed two shows that day and when all was said and done, we were a huge hit. We got "fan mail" from dozens of students, kudos from the other teachers, and I received an offer to stay another year. We even had coverage in the local paper and on the evening news. That was a red-letter day for both my kids and their parents. As for me, it's been more than 25 years since that curtain rose, and I must admit, I often long for the days when life was simple and Raymond Charles Davis was king.

I fell in love with Raymond the second I saw him and believe it or not, I still see him once or twice a year when I visit family and friends in Owego. He is still fidgety and still hilarious, but he now stands about six feet tall and weighs around 250 pounds. He no longer calls me 'Me-Wonant.' It's now 'Wee-Ann.' He loves to reminisce. In fact, when he sees me anywhere on the street, in a store or in church for that matter, he always asks the same question: "Hey Wee-Ann, wemember the time you and your mom took me to the circus and the cannon went off and I got so scared I jumped up and spilled my Coke all over Connie? Wemember that? I was so scared I almost peed! That was funny wasn't it, Wee-Ann?"

I bust out laughing every single time he tells that story. It was perhaps one of the most hysterical and tender moments in my memory. My mom was such a good sport and we *all* laughed so hard we almost peed! Raymond was five and had never been to the circus. He was agog and couldn't keep his eyes off the clowns. We should have known better than to buy him a drink, but he was so adorable and tiny and since he'd never had such an experience, we lavished him with all the glorious decadences the 'Greatest Show on Earth' could provide.

There was a half-eaten candy apple on the seat next to him and popcorn strewn all over the floor. When the cannon went off with a bone-shattering BOOM, he had cotton candy in one hand, and a Coca Cola in the other and yes, he did indeed spill his entire Coke on my mom's head. She laughed harder than anyone. It was a perfect moment and one that will remain etched in my mind as long as I live.

I will never forget you, Raymond Charles Davis.

"Haddy Birdy, buddy…"

> *"The sun, though it passes through dirty places,*
> *yet remains as pure as before…"*
>
> ~Francis Bacon

It was dawn and he was once again awakened by the sound of heavy footsteps hobbling down the hallway toward his room. 'Maybe IT will pass by this morning; maybe IT'S just going to the bathroom.' Wishful thinking turned to terror, and the anticipation of unimaginable agony covered his entire little body like the heavy X-ray blanket the dentist uses.

He rarely slept much. The expectation of impending horror made him restless and vigilant. It wasn't like he could ever escape. He just wanted to be prepared. But like the little white mouse in the terrarium with the python, it can't run, it can't even hide. It can only wait. The bedroom door flew open and slammed against the cheap, dingy press-board wall leaving behind a gaping hole that reminded him of a festering wound. IT stood there in the doorway for a second cocking ITs head from side to side, gloating and mocking ITs prey, like a lion hovering over a wounded gazelle admiring his trophy before he begins to devour it. "Say one fucking word and you won't live to see your sixth birthday, you whiny little bastard," IT bellowed. "You know the routine, get rid of those pajama bottoms and hurry up, goddammit!"

Sunlight began to flood the tiny, cramped tomb-like space through the dirty window. It seemed to hesitate, as if it felt unwelcome, and then proceeded to saturate the room with the glowing promise of a brand new day. His freckled face was buried deep in the pillow, his beautiful red hair drenched with sweat and drool, and he could feel the blood trickling down the back of his leg, drip, drip dripping on the sheets. He'd pay for that later. The burden was overwhelming and the pain unbearable; neither, however, compared to the smell – a rancid cocktail of bad breath, body odor, and the foul stench that rises from the depths of ITS very being. IT collapsed to the floor and lay there like a beached whale, huffing and puffing and wheezing like some sort of sick locomotive.

His baby face was still hidden in his pillow, God forbid IT should catch him crying.

"Now get your whimpering ass up and get ready for school," IT panted with exhaustion. IT staggers back down the dark and smelly hallway, wearing a path on the filthy lime green wall-to-wall carpet. IT felt smug and righteous as IT wallowed in the twisted pleasure of ITs' early morning exploit.

.-.

I sang in the shower that morning and looked forward to another day in the classroom. It was 1985 and I was a 20-something optimist. It was my third year as a Special Education teacher and I was in love with my students. I enjoyed a wonderful rapport with the parents, and as a teacher of children with special needs, it is important to maintain close contact with them and be available to them on a consistent basis. We spent countless hours on the phone, in the classroom and at our kitchen tables plotting new strategies and creating hands-on activities that would enhance the learning process.

As it does every fall, "Meet Your Teacher Night" rolled around. It was on that night that I encountered a young couple who would change my life forever. They were new to the area and clearly a bit mentally challenged themselves. I remember recalling with sadness how the visible signs of abuse hung over the room, like a storm cloud. The wife was a textbook battered woman, and the husband was just plain repulsive.

His eyes darted around the room searching for clues or for answers that would reveal my motive. He spoke in single syllables, and then only when I made casual conversation directly with him. When he did reply, he chose his words very carefully, as if he had silently rehearsed his response many times. Perhaps he believed that I would sense the darkness within. As I continued to probe, feigning innocence, he became increasingly agitated. His poor wife was all too familiar with the tension, and like many victims who fear for their lives on a daily basis, she made a valiant, albeit feeble attempt to sugar-coat the moment. I shut up and surrendered for her sake only.

He gave me the creeps, looking at me with an eerie combination of contempt and desire. His long, stringy, greasy red hair was combed over in a futile attempt to hide the bald spot that consumed the entire circumference of his large head.

His expressionless face looked like a mutant mask that would easily win the Grand Prize in the "scariest" category of a Halloween contest. He walked with a conspicuous limp; it bothered him that I noticed. His looming presence cast a bulky and gruesome shadow over his wife who stood obediently by his side, wilted and lifeless – like a starving, shrinking violet that had been deprived of the sun's warmth and energy for a very long time. She was both pleasant and pitiful, and sincerely concerned with her son's progress. He was eyeballing the cupcakes and didn't care one way or another; his kid was a retard anyway. I see his face sometimes, and after all these years, he still haunts my dreams.

.-.

Every morning without fail it was the same routine. Rain or shine, winter, spring, summer or fall, the little red-haired boy would arrive at school with his belongings tumbling out of his backpack, clothes disheveled, shoelaces untied, with a perpetual case of serious "bed-head." He would wait impatiently until I sat at my desk, which was positioned by the door because that's where he liked it, and the ritual would begin.

It never lasted longer than 30 seconds or so, but a voice deep inside me told me that this sad and troubled little boy needed a diversion, something to look forward to; something predictable and safe and right. He would stand in the hallway anxiously waiting for me to sit at my desk. He would then open the door verrry slooowwly, just a crack, pop his little red head through the opening, grin from ear to ear, and chirp, "Mo-nin' Loance!" No one else had a clue that he was saying "Good Morning, Ms. Lawrence!" and believe it or not, his version of "Lawrence" was incredibly articulate compared to some of the other amusing attempts at my moniker. With a room full of 5-13-year-old mentally and emotionally challenged students, I answered to just about anything. God, I loved those kids.

This particular child, however, both fascinated and frightened me. His cherubic freckled face so innocent and adorable could turn twisted and demonic without warning. At first we weren't certain what would set him off; could have been the weather or maybe one of the other kids, but chairs would fly across the room and he would scratch and kick and bite and curse and his angelic smile would become perverse and distorted until he was barely recognizable.

I was trained to prevent him from harming himself or others, but I was the one who usually required a squirt or two of Bactine and a Band-Aid by the end of the day. I still bear the scars from those chilly fall mornings of 1985, grim souvenirs of good intentions gone bad. Each day I would pray for the strength to deal with the outbursts and for the wisdom to understand them. What was making him so angry? He was only five. What could have been so bad?..

ITs footsteps shuffle slowly down the hall;

IT can sense your fear from the other end of the dark trailer.

IT'S coming...

After weeks of battling the demons that seemed to inhabit his little body, I came up with a much-needed plan. I pored through the educational catalog and finally found what I was looking for. With my own money, I purchased two sets of cardboard people. One represented various careers: a fireman, a doctor, and a nurse, and the other was the All-American family: Dad in his gray suit and tie, mom in her house-dress and apron, and the two kids, a boy and a girl. They were simple props that reminded me of those cheesy photo ops at the carnival where you poke your head through a hole and you're a wild gorilla or the bald-headed strong man wearing a leopard skin and raising barbells over his head with one arm. Sadly, these one-dimensional contraptions would end up creating a much less amusing outcome…

On a dismal winter morning after an intense discussion with Charlene, my Teacher's Assistant, I asked him to skip gym class and do something really fun with us. I told him he would be a movie star. Interestingly enough, he was glad to oblige since he wasn't too crazy about the physical camaraderie typical of contact sports and kindergarten boys. In fact, he didn't like being touched much at all.

In case we needed proof of anything to show to the Department of Children and Families, we had set up a camcorder in the corner of the room. I honestly thought we were prepared. First, he chose the fireman and I got to be the nurse helping him to attend to the injured people he had rescued from the burning building. Poor Charlene, she of course, was one of the victims - paper towel bandages covered her head and were haphazardly held in place with plenty of Scotch tape. A yard-stick splinted her badly 'fractured' arm, and she was sprawled out on the cold tile floor like she had just been hit by a bus. She was a great actress, but I told the 'fireman' that she wasn't being a very good patient, and she didn't follow directions very well either. He thought it was hysterical and was jumping up and down and cheering me on when I insisted that my 'patient' swallow the freshly made Play-Dough' pain-killers' I had made. Even though I assured her they were "for her own good," she deliberately refused my professional advice and kept her mouth clamped shut. For a few wonderful minutes, the three of us sat there on the floor and laughed and laughed. He even curled up in my lap for a brief moment and suggested we try again to get those 'pain pills' into the patient! He had the most beautiful smile.

After he had warmed up to the whole idea of role-playing, I decided it was time to go a step further. I suggested that I be him, and I put my head and arms through the holes of the cardboard son. Then I said, "And why don't you be, oh let's say, your dad?" The transformation took all of about two seconds. As soon as he poked his little red head through the holes of the father figure, he became *IT*. Before I really knew what was happening, I was face down on the floor, held captive by a tiny boy in a harmless piece of cardboard, unable to witness the ghastly manifestation. Charlene's expression was frozen in fear and the shock of the moment had paralyzed her.

I knew it was much worse than I ever could have imagined. I was desperately trying to get my bearings and regain control when he slammed his foot down hard on the back of my head. He was screaming obscenities and ordering me to get my pajama bottoms off and "hurry up goddammit!" When he grabbed me by the hair, Charlene was ready to intervene, but I knew we had to obtain as much proof as possible in order to remove him from the hell in which he was living (or slowly dying), so I waved her off. The next few seconds felt more like hours, and my entire world seemed to be caving in like a sink hole – invasive and gluttonous, swallowing me whole. He was still screaming and drooling and stomping on my back and tearing at my clothes when I decided we had both had enough.

Charlene was all too ready to assist and we removed the suited cardboard father from his flailing little body. Puzzled and exhausted, he looked at me and then at Charlene, almost as if he didn't recognize our faces. He was sweating and panting and afraid he'd done something terribly wrong. He was trying very hard to make some sense of the moment and we stared into each other's eyes seeking answers. Tears were flowing down our cheeks, and our bodies were limp and exhausted from the struggle. Still visibly shaken, he pointed his finger in my direction and began to giggle. He wanted to know what had happened to my hair. Unfortunately, by that time, I was a mess. Not only was my cardboard figure completely destroyed, but I inadvertently bore a striking resemblance to Don King, and we all began to laugh out loud. Relief spilled into the room, like a sudden rain shower, but as expected, it was short-lived and before I could speak, he melted into my arms and began to sob.

It was at that moment that I became aware of the true presence of evil.

He told us what he could remember of those dark and brutal morning attacks and we reluctantly noted the blood stains on his teeny little Fruit of the Looms. We moved quickly and together with the Department of Social Services and he was removed from his parents' home. *IT was furious.*

As we dug deeper into the archives of this family's history, we discovered more disturbing secrets than we were prepared to know. There were others. All four siblings had endured ITs' wrath – his oldest sister had been admitted to a psychiatric facility and labeled "Irreversibly Emotionally Disturbed" just days before her ninth birthday.

By the grace of God and the efforts of a few compassionate people, he was placed in a foster home with a family whom I had known and loved my entire life. They had many children and a strong sense of faith. There was plenty of love to share, and more than enough room in their home and in their hearts for one more. They fell in love with him and he with them. They played in the park, swam in the public pool, helped him with homework, attended church on Sunday and prayed together each night before bed. They wrapped his little body in a blanket of safety and for the first time in his short life, he was happy and privileged and alive. His foster dad's old brief case replaced the worn-out backpack. Every morning as he entered the classroom, he would dutifully inform everyone that he was coming to work. He advised the other kids not to bother him as he removed papers from his attaché because he was busy and had a lot of work to do. He was delightful and diligent. He was silly and oblivious. He was five! His ear-to-ear smile lit up the entire room and we all applauded the change. The Bactine was lost in a drawer, the tension had disappeared, and we welcomed each day with enthusiasm. Every Friday he would dress up in a little tweed jacket and a clip on tie his "new mom" had bought for him. He would beam with pride and his big, brown, fawn-like eyes would sparkle, and I believed at the time that God had created Fridays just for him.

IT was livid. IT sat silently in the darkness of ITs lair and IT schemed. IT would get him back or IT would die trying. IT would be on ITs best behavior and cooperate with the authorities and with the idiots in the fucking Department. IT would do whatever IT had to do to get him back – the rotten little bastard told the secret and let the whole fucking world into their lives. IT will get even.

Unfortunately, IT did.

At that time, the Department of Social Services had a policy that required case workers to schedule an appointment with parents under investigation – no unannounced visits were allowed. This rule gave the accused plenty of time to straighten up a little, run the vacuum, shower, comb their hair, maybe even brush their teeth. *IT knew exactly what to do and what to say to convince the case worker that IT had learned ITs' lesson and that IT was sorry and that IT had changed.* So as the law stated, six months of successful rehabilitation leads to reunification with the natural parents: "All right, buddy, aren't you happy that you're finally going home?"

"Oh my God, IT is going to kill me…*pleeeaaase* don't make me go back there! IT knows everything I said. IT is unforgiving. IT is ruthless. IT *will* draw blood."

He was snatched from a family he had come to love and trust and cherish, and was returned to the filthy, isolated crypt the Department deemed a "suitable environment.*"*

IT was waiting with open arms.

The life form that dragged itself into my classroom just three days later following the 'joyful reunion,' was not the adorable little boy who was dancing around the classroom in a bright red tie on Friday afternoon, but a sickening, disfigured monster - its lifeless eyes staring vacantly into the darkness of its own being.

IT wanted to remind me who was BOSS. IT wanted me to be

afraid.

Doubled over from the pain, his gait was slow and deliberate like that of a shackled hostage. His eyes were black and swollen shut, and his lips were bloated, like drowned cattle. His neck was bruised, and the outline of a large hand was evident in the pale and delicate flesh. Dried blood from his wounds fell to the floor like chipped paint from a condemned building. He had been "reminded" not to open his mouth again. He had surrendered his soul.

I burst into tears when I saw him, so did Charlene. He walked through the door like a zombie and went directly to his chair. There was no cheerful "Mo-nin' Loance!," no grin, no brief case. His innocence was gone, and there was no life left at all. He flinched as he sat down in his chair, the pain obviously excruciating, and he turned his head slowly in my direction and forced me to look into his eyes. The eerie blankness of his stare chilled the blood in my veins, and I sensed hatred in his heart.

He remained slouched over in agony, and like the deformed and hideous hunchback in the old black and white horror films, he frightened the other children. I pretended to be preoccupied, shuffling papers in a futile attempt to reclaim some sense of self-control. I asked Charlene to take the rest of the kids out on the playground for a while. As they gawked through tears at the dreadful, crooked creature they once knew as their friend, they seemed to welcome the opportunity. In single file they left the room in silence, unable to believe their eyes. Trying desperately to stay calm, I knelt down and asked him what had happened.

He didn't melt into my arms this time, he just sat there empty and absent and deflated. His soft Bambi eyes were old and dull, and the pupils were drowning in the bloody broken blood vessels that had submerged them. His hair was matted and clumps were missing, pulled out by the roots. The mean, red welts glared up at me, blaming me. He stared at me through murky, vacant eyes, and without a hint of emotion, sneered at my tear-stained cheeks as if to say, "Mind your own business this time, bitch. Look what you did."

When he finally spoke, his voice cracked because his larynx had been crushed. His tone was no longer whimsical, but lifeless and cold. He had little to say and spoke only five words – words that in any other context would have been trivial. It was those five words that nearly sent me over the edge. My throat closed up and I felt sick. I could feel my heart beating in my temples. Giant beads of sweat mixed with tears, and I tasted the saltiness of my own fear. I suddenly felt helpless and inadequate and small. "Dear God, what had I done? Did I honestly think I could make a lasting difference in his wretched life? How could I have been so arrogant?"

"Honey, can you tell me what happened?"

"I fell off my bike."

In a state of shock, I immediately alerted the Principal, the school nurse, and the local police. There was nothing any of us could do. He had no more to say. The devil had come to call and there was nothing we could do to stop him.

He finished the school year, coming and going back and forth, in and out of the classroom like a duck in a shooting gallery at the county fair. The beautiful little red haired boy was gone, replaced by a catatonic life form that methodically went about its business day in and day out. Not feeling, not really living, wishing it was dead. I had a swimming party at my parent's house on the last day of school. He didn't come. I knew he wouldn't. I never saw him again, but a part of him will forever reside like a ghost in my heart and I will pray for his soul for the rest of my life.

I quit teaching that summer. I nearly had a nervous breakdown. For months I woke up in the middle of the night soaked with sweat and sobbing. For years I imagined a grotesque and deformed figure standing at the foot of my bed cocking his head from side to side. *IT would know when I fell asleep. IT would know when to strike.* Sleep eluded me for a long, long time.

I knew someday I would return to the classroom, but at that time, the summer of 1986, the mere thought of backpacks and bulletin boards made me physically ill. For the next five years I lived, I loved, I laughed, and I traveled, and I tried to forget The Little Red Haired Boy.

Since the day I picked up my first piece of chalk, I have listened patiently to the advice of seasoned, well-meaning educators regarding cases of suspected abuse:

"Don't get involved, sweetie. It'll tear your heart out."

"It will only get you into trouble, kid."

"Oh, sure, right now you want to change the world, but give yourself a few years and you'll settle in. It's just not worth the hassle."

Is a child's life "worth the hassle?" Is it just "too much trouble" to show someone you care enough to "get involved?" Will it even matter in the end? Nelson Mandela once said, "Light a candle or curse the darkness."

In the spring of 1991, my 58 year old mother died of cancer and my world no longer made sense.

Throughout the course of the next 14 years, I tutored and I mentored and I volunteered, but I wasn't ready to go back. I worked in the travel industry for nearly a decade and logged hundreds of miles, racked up countless memories and created lifelong friendships from all over the world. Then I spent two wonderful years working for Challenge Industries in Ithaca, New York, a work-based training facility for folks with varying levels of physical and mental capacity. They used to call places like this Sheltered Workshops, but 'we've come a long way baby.' It was a fascinating job and I believe it was a catalyst of some sort offering me the opportunity to stick my toe back in the water and re-examine my priorities. I loved that place and everyone in it.

So, seeking much needed change, I packed up my worldly belongings and loaded my three old dogs into the back of my buddy Homer's pickup and moved to Florida.

It was 1998. I got a job teaching GED classes to a group of under 18 year old drug offenders who had been court ordered to get their diploma or go to jail. It was there that I learned to be comfortable in my own skin. It was there that I realized where I was supposed to be. It was there that I finally found my footing. And it was there that grace revealed its hidden secrets and collided with my soul.

Now that I'm back, here's my message:
…do what you can
…speak your truth
…love without boundaries or expectations.
…love your work.
…get excited.
…get involved.
…get your hands dirty.
…get quiet.
…go the extra mile.
…go to bat for someone.
…set goals.
…set an example.
…give thanks.
…give everything you've got.
…be loyal.
…be there.
…be brave.
…be strong.
…be real.

...be grateful.
...listen.
...hear.
...smile more.
...laugh a lot.
...hug someone for no reason.
...share.
...reach out.
...reach within.
...cry when you have to.
...pray.
...do what you love.
...do what you can.
...shape up.
...stand up.
...show up.

The Classroom

By far one of the best pieces of advice I've ever received came from a 75-year-old firecracker. She was Jeanne Brannigan, President of the Board for the Ithaca, NY-based Divi Resorts and she was hell on wheels. I was new to the company, so she called me into her office one day to tell me she liked me and that I had "chutzpah." Jeanne said I'd go far if I listened to only one thing she had to say: "Kid, always, and I mean ALWAYS, do something five minutes before you're asked to do it. It's much better to ask for forgiveness than for permission, know what I mean?"

Then she slapped me on the back, removed two etched crystal rocks glasses from her bottom drawer, poured a couple of Cutty Sarks and handed me one. "Here's to ya, kid," she declared as she winked, threw back her scotch, and smiled her beautiful smile. Not long after that conversation, Jeanne lost a long and courageous battle with breast cancer. I'll never forget her.

As a GED teacher in the most disheartening of circumstances, I see and hear things on a daily basis that most people cannot fathom. My students move me. Most walk through my door discouraged and broken, in search of some sense of dignity and purpose. I do my best to see that they feel comfortable, empowered and inspired because upon entering my domain, most students are a nervous wreck. Many haven't been in school in decades, while others are court-ordered to attend. They knock lightly on my door, eyes aimed at the floor, bodies tense and rigid, and I welcome them with open arms, literally. I put my hand out, shake theirs like a long-lost friend, and utter these simple words: "Congratulations! You've just passed the hardest part of this course. You had the guts to walk through that door! The rest is all downhill from here."

They immediately stand up straight, look me square in the eyes for the first time and shake my hand with all the vigor they can muster. The reprieve is obvious and the other students never get enough of that "moment." So I am again, reminded how much I love my job.

It was the first day of class in the fall of 2002, and I was teaching at a One Stop Career Center that housed a Welfare Transition program, a Food Stamps office and many other public assistance programs. As I welcomed all the new and nervous would-be graduates, and delivered my opening homily, I repeated with enthusiasm the words Jeanne had shared with me in 1986. Someone listened.

About a month into the semester on a Friday morning, Tashia timidly raised her hand and asked if she could share something with the class "Absolutely!" I thundered. Of course I had no idea that I was about to experience one of those life-defining moments.

"Well, Miss. Leanne," she began with a shy, sweet smile, flashing four gold front teeth, "do you remember that advice you gave us on the first day of school, when you said we should always do something five minutes before we're asked to do it?"

As I smiled and nodded and waited for her to continue, I noticed the rest of the class sitting up a little straighter. "I wrote it down, right here on this piece of paper," she held it high, like a hard-won Gold Medal at the Olympic Games. "I decided that it sounded pretty good and that I would try it at work for two weeks. So, yesterday, my boss came up to me and said, "Tashia, we've been watchin' you and noticing that you've been doing extra things around here without being told." As the tears welled up in her eyes, she said, "Miss Leanne, they were so impressed that they promoted me to Manager *and* gave me a raise! With six kids, you know that extra little bit will help. And you know what the best part is, Miss. Leanne? My kids are real proud of me!"

So, here's to the management staff at *Checkers*: kudos to you all for recognizing and rewarding those who deserve it.

Here's to you Tashia: may you continue to prosper and raise the bar, and may the example you set for your children continue to inspire them.

And here's to *you,* Jeanne Brannigan: may you rest in peace and know that your influence is eternal.

> *"At the moment of death we will not be judged according to the number of good deeds we have done or by the number of diplomas we have received in our lifetime. We will be judged according to the love we have put into our work…"*
>
> ~Mother Teresa

Since this is a book about my experiences in the educational realm, one would rightfully assume that there would be a section about tests. It would be a helpful segment to provide professional advice and test-taking tips, or possibly one which discussed the secrets of Zen and test anxiety. The truth is, this piece is not as much about tests as it is about cultural diversity and the lessons associated with it.

I believe in tolerance. I believe in each individual's right to express themselves and feel confident doing so. I embrace language in all forms and encourage dialogue on a daily basis. I must sadly admit, however, that I am often ill-prepared to translate the vernacular through which many of my students communicate. According to the experts, the language of "the ghetto," as my students call it, is really quite advanced in a linguistic sense. 'Ebonics' is an entry in *Webster's Dictionary* defined as "a blend of Ebony and Phonics; BLACK ENGLISH." Here are a few examples:

- "noamsayin"?' "Do you know what I'm saying?"
- "lemmeholyopen" "Let me hold your pen." ("Can I borrow your pen?")
- "icanlookatyobook?" "I can look at your book?" ("Can I see your book?")
- "howyougonnatrymelikethat?" "How are you going to try me like that?" ("Why would you challenge me like that?")

I love my work and am grateful to be a part of a culture that thrives on communication and expression. However, here's the irony on which I base this thesis: As is understood, much of the brilliance of Ebonics is that it *reduces* the number of syllables required for a complete sentence or statement, and scrunches them down into a less cumbersome and more advanced utterance. So the first time one of my students

104

actually *added* a syllable to the word "tests," I was admittedly taken aback: "Miss Leanne, do I got to look at any *testes* in here?"

Because I get new students on a daily basis, I've felt the need to create a micro-lesson plan around this occurrence. I go to the board, place the two words side by side and ask if anyone can explain why it matters which one they use. They usually laugh out loud, shake their heads, and assure me that they understand.

Of course it is not my intention to tread upon anyone's cultural morés, but I am compelled to point out the disparity in both the grammar as well as in their pronunciation. Mostly, I feel the need to emphasize the HUGE societal implications – if for no other reason that when interviewing for a job, no one asks the potential employer if he or she will be required to "look at any testes."

"Noamsayin?"

> *"History, despite its wrenching pain, cannot be unlived, but if faced with courage, need not be lived again…"*
>
> ~Maya Angelou

For some reason, I sensed that this Friday morning would be significant. Some call it intuition; others say it's the Holy Spirit tapping you on the shoulder and sending a message straight from God Himself. I kind of like that idea, but either way, I had a feeling that when the day was done, we would all be changed.

Ten of us gathered in my GED classroom that morning, all women in a welfare-transition program, ranging in age from 16 to 62. The communication that crossed generational and cultural boundaries was effortless and free. As usual, Miss Arletta, the elder, sat perfectly composed and erect at the head of the table. She was wearing a lovely floral print dress and seemed to be in good spirits. Apparently her ailing (often miserable) husband was feeling well that morning, so she left the house with a spring in her step. She would be the first to arrive and the last to leave. She'd pull into the parking lot in her old brown car - the one with no air conditioning, no brakes and a tattered Holy Bible on the dashboard.

The first assignment that morning was to read a newspaper article, identify the main idea and write a summary. As I did each day, I selected a story intended to stir emotion and debate. This particular article in *USA Today* focused on a couple of 'white-bread' frat boys from the University of Alabama. It was Halloween and they thought it would be funny to dress up in blackface and dredge up a few horrors from the past. It seems these two arrogant fools staged a mock lynching – one had his face painted black and was kneeling on the ground with his hands tied behind his back and a noose tied loosely around his neck. His buddy was standing proudly behind him in a rented police officer's uniform, grinning from ear to ear while holding a shotgun to his friend's head. Nothing like a little good clean fun, eh? The reaction was the same as each student finished reading. Expressionless faces stared at me in disbelief.

"How could they possibly think that was funny?" one girl whimpered.

The others just shook their heads and became lost in their own thoughts.

As we discussed the concept of lynching, we shared our opinions and purged our anger. Without warning, the disturbing words to Billy Holiday's song *Strange Fruit* invaded my thoughts. I shuddered, and my mind conjured up nightmarish visions of black men with *"bulging eyes and twisted mouths"* hanging from poplar trees throughout the South.

Miss Arletta was noticeably quiet, her posture slumped, and she seemed to be deflating right before our eyes. Sensing her hidden anguish, I was about to bring the discussion to a close when she held up one finger and indicated her desire to speak. She had never done this before, and although I was delighted that she felt comfortable and compelled to share with us, I immediately became aware of the sorrow that had slipped into the room like an uninvited guest. Her voice was shaky at first, as if she were holding back a swollen river of tears. But with conviction and determination, she persevered and before our very eyes, she stepped back in time and brought the horrors of her childhood in rural Alabama into our room like satellite TV.

"White peoples used to throw rocks and bricks and full cans of beer at us when we was kids…" Her delivery was slow and her voice flat and toneless. Her eyes were glazed over and she stared straight ahead, looking directly at no one. It was as if she were watching the events unfold on a big screen somewhere in her mind.

"What do you mean they throwed rocks and bricks at you?" one girl asked with hesitation.

"I means we had to walk miles to get to our little school or to town, and when we passed by the white people's houses or by a white man's store, they throwed things at us and yelled ugly things at me and my sisters."

"Ugly things?" I asked.

She ignored me as if I had asked a ridiculous question. She was right.

"We never knowed what they might do to us neither!" she said, her voice and her body began shaking uncontrollably. We were all on the edge of our seats. I spoke briefly about the violence and corruption and pain endured by blacks in the deep south, and of how the laws favored white people, and how there was simply no justice if you were black.

Arletta didn't even realize she had interrupted me when she continued, "Three white mens took my baby sister into the woods one Sunday when we was walkin' home from church."

No one was certain if she planned to continue, but it wouldn't have mattered anyway. None of us could move.

"They tore her up so bad, she could never have chil'ren of her own."

She was gazing into the emptiness of her own heart and wallowing once again in the terror of the moment.

"Ever'body knowed who they was. Peoples even saw them snatch her up and drag her off, a-kickin' and a-screamin', but nobody said nothin', nobody *did* nothin'. Those mens that took her and ruined her, they heared we said somethin' to the po-lice, so they came to our house aimin' to teach us a lesson. It was just my mama and us kids there at the house, and they came up in they old beat up trucks and they was just a-hollerin' and a-yellin'. Then they started poundin' nails and, Miss Leanne, they boarded us up inside and was fixin' to burn that house down with us in it!"

We were frozen in our seats. I could barely breathe.

"That's when my daddy came home. He got out of his truck totin' his shot gun and threatenin' to use it on any man who struck a match! Those mens rode off cussin' and sayin' they'd be back to finish the job, but we never heared another thing from 'em – never had no more trouble…no more trouble." To this very day my sister ain't right. She ain't never married, and she still skeered of mens too…"

I struggled hard to find the words to bridge the gap between those terrifying images of the 1940s and the reality of sitting in my classroom in 2001. It didn't matter though; she wasn't finished.

"They came and got my uncle in the middle of the night," she muttered almost incomprehensibly. Her hands were folded in her lap, her head was down, and her eyes were closed, like she was in some sort of a trance.

"What do you mean?!" asked one of the younger girls, not really wanting an answer.

"I means he didn't do nothin' wrong and they busted down his door and took him away."

"Took him where?" another girl ventured.

"To 'da 'hangin' tree'" she said matter-of-factly.

"They cut him up before they hanged him, too. Even cut off his private parts. Then they strung him up, still a-kickin' and a-bleedin' everwhere! Dear Lord," she wailed, "them peoples even brought they chil'ren to watch! Miss Leanne, they had picnic baskets and was sittin' on the lawn on quilts!" When it was over, they cut off his head and threw it in a ditch."

A palpable sense of dread hung over the room like an angry storm cloud about to burst.

"Ever'body, includin' the po-lice watched, and nobody did nothin' to stop it. Nobody ever got into no trouble neither."

"How old were you then, Arletta?" I asked quietly.

"I was nine years old."

Tears were flowing freely and words of comfort would not come, but before anyone could catch their breath, she shook her head and in a tone I did not recognize she said, "My husband used to beat me bad."

I didn't know how much more we could take, but she continued and we had no choice but to listen.

"Peoples got married young back then. My man took to drinkin' and got mean. I had two chil'ren, a boy and a girl. I couldn't take no more of the beatin', so I took my egg money and I packed up my babies and got us on a bus. We went as far as we could and got off that bus in the dark of the night. I didn't know nobody, didn't even know where we was, so I sat in that bus station with my babies until the sun come up. I didn't have no money to buy us no food or nothin', so I sat there holding by babies and prayed to God to take care of us. That mornin', a nice lady came right up to me sittin' on that bench with two babies, and asked what was I doin' there. I said I didn't know for sure. I just had to get out. She took us in and gave us a place to stay. Miss Leanne, I think she was an angel sent right from God. We stayed with her almos' two years. I got a job cleanin' houses and she wouldn't never take no money from me. She said to take that money and buy our food and our clothes and such. To this very day, she be in my prayers every night – don't know what we would've done without her, Lord knows, Miss Leanne, Lord knows."

She paused again, almost as if she was gathering her strength to go on. Somehow I knew the next chapter wouldn't be the 'Happily Ever After' we were all hoping for.

"We moved back down here when I heered my husband was sick. I moved back in with him to take care of him, only the Lord knows why, but I did. My kids was runnin' wild and my man couldn't do nothin' about it, and maybe I was tired of fightin'.

She stared off into the distance and tears began to stream down her cheeks. "When my daughter was 13, she got bad into the drugs," she said.

Looking sharply into the eyes of every girl in the room she repeated herself: "Real bad. She wouldn't come home for weeks at a time, and I never knowed if she was dead or alive mos' times."

"That had to be hell," I said.

"It was the devil's works, Miss Leanne! One day when she came home all raggedy and doped up, I tol' her to git and not come back until she got off the drugs. It was the hardest thing I ever done, but it had to be – it just *had* to be…" Her voice trailed off and she was almost whispering as she stared straight ahead and nodded repeatedly doing her best to justify that painful decision in her own heart.

"Next time I seen her, she was married and had a little baby girl. Her man had just got out of prison for killin' another man. He was mean, awful mean. My daughter was still on the drugs and looked real bad. Me and her man didn't see eye to eye, so he took her off someplace. By the time she came roun' agin, she had another baby girl. I remember axin' her why those poor babies was always bruised up, and she would try to tell me they was just clumsy and to min' my own business. I knew she was lyin', but if I said too much, I wouldn't get to see my grandbabies!"

She was shaking. Arletta's only daughter died of a heroin overdose at age 24. Her innocent little girls, ages two and three, were left in the care of a demon.

"The neighbors, they heered all the screamin'," she said, seemingly leaving her body and sitting there motionless like a zombie. "He was killin' those babies! They tried to break down the door, but he wouldn't let nobody in, so they called the po-lice. By the time the po-lice got there and broke the door down, that two-year-old baby girl was layin' there in a pool of blood – dead!"

He burnt her and beat her so bad with a flatiron, they couldn't even tell what she looked like befo! Her older sister was hidin' behind the door a-screamin' and a-yellin' and a-prayin' to God as loud as she could. She told the po-lice he was a-comin for her next. He was tellin' her to shut up and that he couldn't take no more or her yellin' and that God wasn't goin' to help her no how!"

Her eyes were vacant and her hands were once again folded neatly in her lap. "The po-lice got him befo' he could get to the three-year-old, thank the Lord above. They threw him in jail, and do you know, he was out in three years?

Yessir, and he wasn't out on the street a month befo' he robbed a dry cleaner and kilt that man and his wife both dead. He ain't never gonna git out now," she said with satisfaction and a faint smirk.

The girls were exhausted. We all sat in silence and prayed there would be no more, at least not on this day. They looked into my eyes desperately searching for answers or some sort of clue as to what they should do or how they should react. There were no answers, and while Miss Arletta was still lost in the past, I silently thanked God for everything I had. I believe she knew she was loved. I believe she knew that she was safe. And I believe she knew that moment, as she had known her whole life, that God works in mysterious ways. In my heart, I felt she needed to say all of those things out loud. I wondered if she ever had before. It was important to her that someone understood who she was and how far she had come. More than anything, I believe in ways she may never know, she changed our lives forever... Bless you, Miss Arletta.

Strange Fruit

[Written especially for Billie Holiday by Lewis Allan]

Southern trees bear strange fruit
Blood on the leaves and blood at the root
Black bodies swinging in the southern breeze
Strange fruit hanging from the poplar trees
Pastoral scene of the gallow south
The bulging eyes and the twisted mouth
Scent of magnolia sweet and fresh
Then the sudden smell of burning flesh
Here is a fruit for the crows to pluck
For the rain to gather, for the wind to suck
For the sun to ripe, for the tree to drop
Here is a strange and bitter crop

> *"May I never find myself yawning at life…"*
>
> ~Toyohiko Kagawa

Remember the verse of an old nursery rhyme that goes, "A Butcher, A Baker, and A Candlestick Maker?" Well, in my case, it's more like "A Fugitive, A Stripper, and An Illicit Money Maker!" Welcome to my world. My life as a GED teacher is incredibly rewarding. At times, it's also extremely entertaining.

A Fugitive

To get your attention, sometimes they hiss. It sounds like a sudden puncture in a bicycle tire. It's kind of weird, actually, but what's even odder, is that I respond. I got out of my car in front of the local high school for which I worked in north central Florida, and as I made my way into the front office, I heard a slow, deliberate "hisssss," followed by a low whisper, "Hissssssss - Miss Leanne!"

I craned my neck a bit but didn't recognize any of the cars parked out front, so I kept on walking. "Miss Leanne – over here – hissssssss!"

"Well, for the love of God, Meatball, where on earth have you been, and why are you all crumpled up and hiding in this car?"

"Shhhh, Miss Leanne, I just had to leave town for a little minute. Can I still come back to class?"

"A little minute? I haven't seen you in almost a month! And yes, you know you can always come back. You look awful – haven't you been eating?"

"Yes ma'am, I been eatin'. Thanks – I'll see you Friday, Miss Leanne. Oh, hey, do you think I can get a ride home after class?"

"Who are you '50-Cent' and I'm your limo driver?"

He grinned. I shook my head and rolled my eyes, "You know I'll take you home just so I can talk to your mama!"

"Okay 'den – see you Friday." He nodded to the female driver and I watched them drive away.

"I won't hold my breath," I yelled. He laughed out loud and waved goodbye.

As I walked into the front office, I felt the tears burning in my eyes. I worry about them like they're my own. Here's a kid who would give you the shirt off his back if he thought you needed it. He always carried a wad of cash rolled neatly in his pocket – had to be at least five hundred bucks on any given day. He'd been dealing drugs since he was seven years old. He had a good heart and always offered to pay for my gas when I took him home, asking if I needed anything.

"Hey, I know teachers don't make no money. Can I buy you a soda, Miss Leanne?"

"No thank you!" I would say smirking, but totally serious. "Not with *that* money!" "Oh, comeonnow, Miss Leanne, it spends like any money!"

"I just happen to know where it came from, honey; thanks, but no thanks!"

"But I got me a job at 'da WalMart, Miss Leanne, you know 'dat…"

"Sweetie, there are Board members at Wal Mart who don't carry as much cash as you do!"

He would shrug his shoulders, shake his head, and throw his hands in the air. "You is off 'da chain, Miss Leanne!"

He was one of the sweetest kids I had ever met. He was a textbook victim of a culture that would fail him time and time again. It's been six months and no one has seen him.

A Stripper

As I was rifling through papers during class the other day, I came across a registration form that I had never turned in. I remembered this girl. She came in on the first day like many of them do, all gung-ho and ready to make a huge life change.

"I needs to get my GED so I can set a good example for my kids!" she declared.

"Good for you," I cheered. "You've come to the right place; see you in the morning!"

I never saw her again. It's pretty typical, but we persevere because we live and hope that they'll come back.

When I asked my girls if they knew her, not even two decades of experience could have prepared me for their response: "Oh, Miss Leanne, you mean '*TableTop?*'"

"*Table Top?*" I asked.

"You know, 'TableTop.' She a stripper, Miss Leanne!"

"Oh for God's sake – a stripper? Well, does she make a decent living?"

"You is funny, Miss Leanne! She ain't no professional stripper. She claim to be one of them exotic dancers. But shit, I only ever knowed her to dance on da tables at parties and such!"

"At parties? Well, I don't get it – who comes to a party with a stash of dollar bills?"

"Oh, she don't make no money doin' it, Miss Leanne! Oh, maybe a dolla or two. She just do it just 'cuz she like to do it! She like da attenshun! Ain't you never heered of dat befo, Miss Leanne?"

"Well, actually, no. I'm pretty sure I've never been to a party where a woman just jumped up on a table and started taking off her clothes. Guess I've led a sheltered life."

They were howling. "You is somethin' else, Miss Leanne! Maybe you needs to get out mo'!"

"Why on earth would I want to go to parties like that?"

"We just *gots* to take you clubbin', Miss Leanne! You would be off 'da chain!"

I can hardly wait.

An Illicit Money Maker

It was a typical Tuesday morning and this particular young man had arrived late as usual. It was my observation that his goal was really not to learn anything new, but to socialize and to brush up on his trade. He wanted to be a hair dresser. While eating some sort of snack item, he was braiding Tammy's hair and declaring his overwhelming desire to get out of GED class and into cosmetology school.

"'Scuse me, Miss Leanne," he interrupted a one-on-one session I was conducting with another student. "'Scuse me, let me ask you a serious question: Why do you think my test scores aren't improving? Damn! I need to get this over with so I can get into Cosmetology School!"

His intrusion was nothing new, so without looking up or blinking an eye, I nonchalantly answered, "Well, I don't know, sweetie. It's probably because you're lazy." He squealed and gasped, and slapped poor Tammy on the head. *LAZY*?" he said huffing and puffing and seeking solidarity from the girls. "Can you *believe* what she just said?"

His hands were on his hips and he was short of breath. His mouth was wide open but the words would not come. The girls were cracking up. He glared at them seeking some sort of support. Surely *some*one had to think I was evil! They looked at him, shrugged their shoulders and shook their heads. Rubbing *her* sore head, Tammy said grinning, "Well, if da shoe fit!"

Distraught and betrayed, he stormed out of the room and slammed the door. He never returned to class and the girls said he was so mad he didn't care if he got his diploma or not. He said "he could do hair out of his grandma's house, SHIT! I don't need no *damn* diploma to cornrow!"

About six weeks later, I was sitting in traffic listening to the news and heard that a local 16-year-old boy had been arrested for extortion. As I always do when I listen to the radio, watch the local news or read the newspaper, I paid a little more attention to the specifics, name, age, etc. because the chances are pretty good that it's a student of mine. Unfortunately, I was right.

The reporter continued saying that the boy had posed as an adult on the Internet and had been communicating with a 25-

year-old man from up north. Apparently, according to the report, the two found that they had a great deal in common, and the boy asked the man to e-mail him some nude photos. The man obliged; the boy received the pictures, and then revealed his true age. The boy then ordered the man to send him money or he would call the police and report the man as a sexual predator. Twenty-five hundred dollars later, the man contacted the local police department and asked for their help. The boy was arrested when an undercover cop pretended to be the man from the north. That night every one of my girls called me at home asking, "Ooh, Miss Leanne, did you hear about Antwan?!"

The next morning, I pulled into the career center where I teach Adult Education three days a week. There was a lone car in the parking lot with two people in it. Since I was usually the first one there, I paid close attention. The door opened slowly and a young man got out wearing a sweatshirt with the hood up. I became more vigilant and stayed close to my car, just in case, but as he came closer, I noticed that his hands were in his pockets, and his head was down. He looked disheartened, and I knew right away it was him. Before he could speak, I smiled, hugged him hard and asked, "Where have you been, sweetie? It's really good to see you!"

He squeezed me so hard I lost my breath for a second. His grandmother got out of the car and came toward us. She looked a little nervous until I hugged her as well and said, "Thank you for bringing him back. He's so close to getting his diploma but I thought I'd lost him forever."

She stood up a little straighter and with her pride in tact, she looked deep into my eyes, and in those few seconds, I saw a lifetime of struggle. I saw the pain and frustration of having to raise her grandchildren. I saw a quiet strength that comes only from a deep sense of faith. "Thank you," she said quietly, then looked at the boy. "I've got to get to work now, Antwan. You buckle down and do what your teacher say!"

"Yes, ma'am," he said grinning broadly.

I knew that his Probation Officer told him he'd better beg to be allowed back into GED class because if he didn't, he would go to jail. I knew how hard it was for him to get out of that car. I understood the epidemic of grandparents raising their grandkids in a culture gone awry.

'Buckle down,' he did. The rest of the students welcomed him back and encouraged his every effort. For the next month, he worked his tail off. He came in on time every morning, completed all of his assignments and passed the Pre-GED tests with flying colors. He had been given a second chance and he took full advantage of it. He took the GED and began working on his community service hours.

A couple of months later during my morning class, I received an "urgent" phone call. The receptionist popped her head in and said, "I'm so sorry to interrupt your class, Leanne, but a young man said he just *had* to speak with you."

"Hello, Miss Leanne, it's Antwan," he said trying to sound so professional.

"Hey you, what's up?!"

"Well, not much. I just wanted to say thank you. Thank you for everything!"

"Thank me, for what, honey?"

"Miss Leanne," he squealed, "I passed my GED and I've been accepted into Cosmetology School!"

I could hear him grinning.

> *"I'd rather die standing than live on my knees..."*
>
> ~Shania Twain

She was probably in her late forties, but looked a lot older, and I remember wondering what she had endured in her lifetime, and how she had finally mustered enough courage to cross that threshold into my Adult Education classroom. She was rail thin with light blonde, shoulder-length hair. Her two front teeth were missing, and it was obvious that she was extremely self-conscious. When she spoke, she did her best to cover the gap with her thin lips. Sometimes she used the back of her hand to cover her mouth, and she constantly looked to the floor as though she couldn't bear to witness a reaction. She was soft-spoken and timid. She tried so hard to make eye contact, but she kept her head down as if she didn't feel worthy. She said she was embarrassed because she was only coming to class because she had to. (I worked with members of the Welfare Transition Program and GED was on their list of options with which to fulfill their requirements.)

"I'm a terrible person and I'm awful ashamed that I didn't stay in school in the first place," she looked around the room at the younger girls and hung her head. "I know I should be coming here because I *want* to, but it's just that I'm working so hard to get my kids back," she said with conviction in her tone. "I'll do whatever it takes, Miss Leanne; my kids mean more than anything in the world to me."

I already wanted to hug her and tell her that she was safe and that no one was going to hurt her on my watch, but I realized it was too soon. I thought of the furry little creature you see abandoned and terrified in your back yard. It never fails that if you try too hard to help it, it just scoots off into the bushes never to be seen again. No one likes to admit it, but the neighbor's cat usually gets it. Something told me that if I tried too hard on this day, I would lose her forever.

The entire class welcomed her with open arms. In fact, they actually embraced her as she searched for an open seat. It was as if most of them saw their own mothers in this frail and frightened woman who was sacrificing, actually begging for another chance to be a better mom. During the next couple of days, she grew more and more comfortable and confident and kept looking at me as if she had something to say. As I strive to do on a daily basis, I did my best to create and maintain a welcoming, tolerant environment, one in which people feel empowered and hopeful and safe.

"My ex-boyfriend did this to me," she blurted out one dismal, muggy morning.

We all knew she was talking about the missing teeth and the fractured cheekbones. None of us was surprised; we just listened.

"He used to beat me bad…he's the reason I lost my kids. No!" she corrected herself, "*I'm* the reason I lost my kids," she said shaking her head violently. "I put up with all the hitting, and I believed all the lies. I actually had the guts to put him in jail for it once, but…"

Suddenly, with a quick jerk, she reeled around and looked behind her. Her eyes darted around the room as if she was making sure he wasn't there lurking in the shadows. I sensed that she wanted to continue.

"But, Miss Reba?" I offered.

"Oh yeah, sorry, but he got out and hunted me down. He beat me unconscious. He said if I told anyone or ran again, he would kill me. Miss Leanne, he said he would kill us all! So in the middle of the night, when he was passed out from drinkin', I gathered up my kids and everything I could fit in a paper bag and I left. The kids was asleep and I had to carry all three of them out to the car. I had an old junker that started sometimes, but most times it didn't. Miss Leanne, I don't know if I ever prayed so hard in my whole life. My heart was poundin' and the kids was startin' to wake up. I asked God to please let the car start, please just this one last time so I can get to the police station."

The rest of the class was on the edge of their seats and doing their best to hold back tears of pain and rage. They had nervously begun the ritual of shuffling papers and tapping their pens. Most of them were all too familiar with her story – most of them had been through it.

"Well, Miss Leanne, God was with us that night. The car started and the policemen were real nice. I told them what had happened, and they asked if I wanted to go to the hospital for my cuts – they was pretty deep 'cause he wore a big Marine Corps ring. I told them I had been through worse, and they helped me get to a shelter in another county. They told me not to tell another soul where we were. They said our lives depended on it. When they was sure we was safe, they went to the house and arrested him. Well, I had to tell my mom and my best friend where we was, but I didn't tell no one else."

"When he got out, he was real mad. He bought himself a used suit and went knockin' on the doors of all our old friends sayin' how he had changed – how he found The Lord while he was locked up. He was about to give up, knowin' he wasn't welcome at my best friend's house, but he went anyway. He was real desperate. She wasn't gonna let him on the porch, but she said he looked real nice and real clean and that he even got a haircut and shaved his beard. When he asked her if I finally moved to St. Augustine, she was pretty surprised. He said I had always talked about movin' there 'cause I loved the water and all the old buildings and such. She thought I must have talked to him, 'cause that's exactly where I was, but I never told nobody I ever wanted to live there. I guess he was smarter than anybody gave him credit for, 'cause without meanin' to do us any harm, my girlfriend sent him right to us."

Our eyes were fixed on her slight frame, her sad eyes, and her misshapen face. We felt helpless...no one could move.

"I was on the phone when he burst through the door," she said as her voice cracked and her eyes glazed over. It was as if she had left her body right there in front of us. I pictured

Jack Nicholson in the movie *The Shining,* the part where he was wielding an ax and cackling, "Heeeeere's Johnny!"

I shuddered.

"Before I really knew what was happening, he was bashing my face in with the phone. I remember seeing blood, tasting blood, and I remember thanking God that the kids was in school. He kept raising his hand and I saw blood dripping from the cord, and that's about all I remember. I woke up in the hospital more than a week later."

We were all short of breath and our hearts were pounding. She was so meek and sweet and helpless, what kind of an animal could raise a hand, much less a weapon, to her? Unfortunately, we all knew was coming, and the other girls began to cry.

"The first thing I did was ask for my kids," she continued as she came out of her trance. Tears welled up in her eyes, but she defied them and held them back. It was as if she had fallen victim to them too many times before and was not about to let them betray her now.

"The nurse said to calm down and rest and not to worry about them right then. I said, 'Where are my babies? Please God tell me he didn't get to them!'"

The nurse said she didn't know but she would have someone come in and talk to me. I said I didn't want to talk to nobody but my kids! Where are my kids?"
The state of Florida had taken her children and placed them in Foster Care.

Three years later, after enduring the humiliation of surrendering her soul and all the intimate details of her private life to representatives of the state, she was so close to getting them back. She was to appear in court the next day. Her fate and the fate of her family rested in the hands of a single judge. I prayed he'd be fair and compassionate and that he would see how hard she was trying. I prayed that he wouldn't get up on the wrong side of the bed or have an argument with his wife before breakfast.

"Like I said before, I'm awful ashamed that I've been comin' here just to get my kids back, but Miss Leanne, tomorrow's the big day, the day I've been dreamin' of for three long years."

Her head was down and the tears were flowing freely.

"Don't you *ever* be ashamed of trying to be a good mother, Miss Reba," I said from the bottom of my heart. "These young girls should be taking notes!"

She looked at me with sincere disbelief and heartfelt appreciation, and for the first time in the month that she'd been attending class, she hugged me. She hugged me hard and thanked me for making her feel like she could be herself. I looked into her blue eyes that seemed brighter and more hopeful than ever before and said, "God be with you in court tomorrow, Reba; you'll be in my prayers."

"I'll need all the prayers I can get!" she replied with the shaky voice of uncertainty. "I'm so nervous. I probably won't get any sleep tonight!"

Then my girls once again proved to me that the meaning of life can be found in the simple notion of sisterhood. "You know *we'll* be prayin' for ya too, Miss Reba!" they said in unison.

Then without hesitation, each girl lined up and embraced her as if she was their own mother heading into battle just for them. It really was remarkable.

Less than 24 hours later, she burst through the door of my classroom – highly unlike her, but exhilarating all the same. "I got my kids back! After all this time, they're really coming home!"

We all sobbed shamelessly and held each other tight. It's been five years and I haven't seen her since that day. I believe she's been doing her best to become reacquainted with her own children. I believe she'll forgive herself one day. I believe they'll make it. And I believe with all my heart that her

children are truly blessed.

> *"We do not remember days, we remember moments..."*
>
> ~Casare Pavese

Ever since I was a little kid, I've had a hard time eating anything if I am uncertain of its origin. I know it sounds a bit absurd, but if I've never seen your kitchen, I ain't eatin' it. I place partial blame on my dear old Aunt Barb – my mom's younger sister and one of the funniest people I've ever known. Aunt Barb became like a mom to me after Connie died, and I'll be forever grateful to her for that.

We came from a pretty good sized family. Aunts, uncles and cousins would fill the seats at my Gradma Bennett's dining room table every Sunday. She would bake homemade yeast-rising rolls from scratch, and everyone brought a dish to pass. We ate like kings, and after dinner, my grandfather would sit in the living room, haul his old fiddle from its case, and play for us kids as we gathered around his chair. Mine was an awesome childhood, filled with laughter, family stories, music and love.

My minor food phobia started on the occasional weekend when we would travel to a different relative's home for Sunday dinner. Dressed in our Sunday best, our moms would pile us into the car, and carefully pack their home made masterpieces: macaroni and cheese, baked beans, scalloped potatoes, and various other steaming, bubbling concoctions into cardboard boxes painstakingly lined with newspaper and towels to keep them hot and to avoid spillage. "Keep an eye on those potatoes," she would say, "I don't want the car smelling like cream of mushroom soup!" I didn't care if it did. I was too busy squirming at the thought of having to 'try everything on my plate.'

As we arrived at our destination, I was immediately whisked to the 'children's table' to join my cousins. I knew what was coming: Connie would place a firm hand on my shoulder and discreetly tell me to "try everything - you don't have to eat it all, but put a little dab of each thing on your plate so you don't hurt anyone's feelings…" UGH. I must admit, as much as I loved my family, I often questioned the integrity of many a dish – I had some interesting cousins who would insist on licking the spoon *before* my aunts were done mixing! ICK…I tried not to think about it. No such luck. Aunt Barb saw me staring blankly at the tiny blobs of food placed neatly on my plate so they didn't touch. She knew I was in hell so she nonchalantly strolled over and whispered "I know how you feel, sweetie. You never know if you're eating 'booger soup!'" *'What?! Booger Soup?!,'* "Mom – I'm full!" "Honey, you haven't even picked up your fork. Now stop being rude and at least give that scalloped corn a try." Aunt Barb would chuckle under her breath, Connie would roll her eyes, and Bennett family history would be made.

Fast -forward to the year 2000. As a new and optimistic GED teacher in a Welfare Transition Program in central Florida, I was ready to change the world. My students ranged in age from 16 to 72 and I was in heaven. Some were court-ordered to be there, while others were just trying to get their lives back on track and do better for their families.

As the fall semester progressed and my students both amazed me and empowered me, we became like a family. Thanksgiving was fast approaching, and someone suggested that we have a party. "You know, Miss Leanne, some of 'dese folks won't get no decent meal for the holiday, so let's make sure 'dey get one here!" I find it amazing that even those who have next to nothing will share what they have with those who have less...God Bless them.

"Oh, I don't know," I said hesitantly... *'booger soup...'* "I'm not much of a chef and I don't want to put anyone else on the spot - what if some people don't have anything to bring?" "We got it covered, Miss Leanne," Donna chirped. "If you'll just get some fried chicken from the Publix, we'll work around that!" "O.K.," I sighed, "I'll get plates and napkins and some drinks too." "That'll be great!," Tiffany assured me, "we'll take care of the rest, Miss Leanne!" Maybe I'll be alright, I thought, I'll just eat whatever comes in a package from the store.

The big day arrived and boy did these people know how to party! There were ribs and salads and casseroles of every kind. There was home-made corn bread and red velvet cake. The room smelled wonderful and people from the rest of the building wandered in. "We've got plenty," I offered. "Feel free to dig in!" As I mingled about, a palpable sense of joy blanketed the room and I again marveled at the remarkable tenderness of the human spirit. My sense of nirvana was pierced by Donna's sweet, albeit loud voice telling me I was in for a big surprise...oh dear God, I thought.! "Miss Leanne, Miss Arletta has spent the past two days preparing the best pot of greens I've ever tasted!" "She shore did," SanSan piped in, "and we saved the best part just for you!"

"Oh, come on now, you guys," I said nervously, "uh, what could possibly be better than what I've already eaten?" "You like collards?," Miss Arletta asked proudly. "Well, uh, I don't know that I've ever had them. What *are* collards exactly?" The room filled with laughter and Miss Arletta waved for them to pipe down. "Miss Leanne, collards are greens, like cabbage and such, and 'dey got a real good flavor if you cook 'em with the right 'gredients." "Oh, I like cabbage," I stuttered, "but what exactly are the 'right ingredients'?" "You sho' is funny, Miss Leanne!" "'Dey is secret 'gredients! Been in my family for years and years. Now you just sit down and enjoy!"

I don't think I would have been so nervous if the entire class hadn't surrounded me like a posse as I sat alone in the middle of the huge table with an empty plate in front of me. "No paper plates for collards, Miss Leanne," Arletta stated matter-of-factly, "'dey is real messy but 'dey is reeal good!" The whole class cheered as she ladled the first pile of dripping greens onto my plate. "You is gonna love this, Miss Leanne!," Tiffany beamed. "Not everybody gets 'dis kinda privilege!" *Gulp*.

What happened next is almost indescribable. The second helping hit my plate with a loud and piercing 'CLUNK.' "What the…..?!" I nearly leapt out of my seat. By now the class was applauding Miss Arletta's culinary prowess – me, I was trying not to barf. Lying there in a bed of limp collard greens was a giant pig's foot, skin and all… "See, Miss Leanne," they shouted, "see how lucky you is?!" *"But it's the foot off of some poor pig,"* I said in despair. *"And it still has a* **hoof** *on it,"* I whimpered. *"What on earth am I supposed to do with it?"* They were doubled over laughing. Surely this was a prank, I thought, but why were most of them were drooling?!

"Really, why don't you take it, Miss Arletta. I know you've been cooking for days and days, it's only right that you should get the bounty (or the hoof)!" With unfettered glee she squealed, "is you **sure**, Miss Leanne? I saved it just for you!" "Oh now, Miss Arletta, that's so kind, but you know I'm not a big eater and besides, I honestly wouldn't know where to begin! Maybe you can show me how it's done!" Relief washed over me like a cold shower as she pulled up a chair, stuffed a napkin in her dress and scooped up the errant limb. Then with reckless abandon, she began to gnaw on the skin, tearing at it like a hyena. "You see? You eats them just like chicken feets! You've had them before haven't you, Miss Leanne?" I must have been green because by that time, Donna was frantically fanning me with a paper plate and Tiffany was nervously dabbing at my forehead with a wet paper towel. I didn't faint or even gag, but they whisked me out of the room like paramedics and got me some much-needed air.

As I stood in front of the building looking at these two awesome women who grew up knowing just what to do when someone you love is in trouble, I smiled and hugged them both. Within seconds we busted out laughing and twelve years later whenever I see either one of them, we reminisce, we smirk, and we shake our heads. "You'll have to put that in your book someday, Miss Leanne," they always say.

Here it is, girls – I will never forget you.

The County Jail

"Give light and the darkness will disappear of itself..."

~Erasmus

"Did somebody paint these?" he asked, fascinated.

"Uh, yeah, God!" Eric replied with a smirk. "No, really, why is they so many different colors?" "'Cuz that's how they come, man, damn, ain't you never seen a seashell before?!" "No," he said, still marveling over the bunch of shells I had dumped out on the table. "And I ain't never been to the beach befo' neither," he said looking off into the distance and fondling the shells like they were made of pure gold. "Shit, man! You live in Florida and you ain't never seen the ocean? Damn, what rock you been livin' under?!"

"Ain't no rock nowhere. Just tryin' to raise my son, man. Just tryin' to do the right thing by my family..." He was 16.

"Lick the tip of your finger, Larry," I said quietly. "Oh my goodness, Miss Leanne!," he grinned, "I taste salt!" "You've seen it in pictures and in the movies, but now you know what the ocean actually *tastes* like…" He beamed.

It was the fall of 2002 and I was teaching GED at the county jail in central, Florida. This was my class for juvenile offenders. They were young boys who had committed very serious crimes and both were facing time in adult prison.

They would be with me for nearly a year and would become like Sherpa Guides in the Himalayas. I was the optimistic white girl from the north who had immersed herself in a dark and dangerous world. They wanted to protect me, to shepherd me over the treacherous terrain, up the perilous, winding footpath that led to the end of the trail – a shadowy place obscured by poverty and prejudice - a final destination that boasted no summit and afforded no revelry. I would be forever changed…

> *"Whoever fights monsters should see to it that in the process* he does not become a monster…"
>
> ~Nietzsche

He was kind and polite and respectful. He was a born leader. The other juvenile boys at the county jail looked up to him. He was articulate and conscientious and could carry on an intelligent and enjoyable conversation. He chose his words carefully and avoided the dialect of his own culture. Many of the other boys who grew up in the projects communicated on a more physical level, gyrating and flailing their hands in the air like 'gansta rappers' on the BET channel. They would ramble on and on and on in a language I barely knew, and inevitably complete each sentence with *"YouknowwhatI'msayin'?"*

I must admit, I thought it was kind of funny that they really expected me to *"know what they were saying."* He would smirk, shake his head, roll his eyes, and politely translate their slang. I liked him and I trusted him. He had the sweetest smile.

"'Come into my parlor,' said the spider to the fly…"

I remember trying to imagine why he was there – why such a nice kid was behind bars. When you work with inmates of any age, you learn quickly about boundaries, and I have always done my best to acknowledge and respect them. Thus, if a person wanted me to know what he or she had been charged with, they shared it with me; otherwise, I simply did not ask. It wasn't until a few weeks after he had been transferred to a state juvenile facility that I found out the truth. My two remaining students spoke freely of his offense and assumed that I had read his file. I was shocked and humiliated and appalled. I was ashamed and totally disappointed in myself for letting my guard down. As I sat in the classroom that day with my remaining students, I remember staring off into space and I began to cry. *"Man, Miss Leanne, I'm sorry, I thought you knew,"* Eric said sincerely. *"No,* I had no idea! If I had known why he was in here, I probably wouldn't have been so damn nice to him!"

Before the last word tumbled recklessly from my lips, I was suddenly and acutely aware of the fact that I should have been very afraid. Had I become *'the monster?'*

Both boys were confused and unsure how to deal with my anxiety. I repeated myself as if I hadn't spoken the words at all. My own disturbing statement had no effect on me, and nothing made sense. The room was spinning and I was sick to my stomach.

"Dammit, you guys, I had no idea!" I said too loudly as I stood up from the table and overturned my chair. "Why didn't someone *tell* me? I *definitely* wouldn't have been so nice to him!"

Eric shifted in his chair and avoided eye contact, but he was adamant. In a calm voice, he spoke the words that both soothed my soul and caused me great shame at the same time: "Yes, you would have, Miss Leanne. That's just who you are."

I was raised to give everyone the benefit of the doubt.

I was raised to believe that respect is a two-way street.

I was raised to consider all sides of the story before making a decision.

I was raised to be decent and tolerant and approachable.

I was raised to believe that we must be kind because everyone is fighting their own difficult battle.

The State of Florida said he raped a two-year-old girl.

As responsible adults and committed educators, is it okay of us to be openly outraged at the actions of others? When do we know that we've reached our limit and that it's time to find another line of work? When is it socially acceptable to stand up and yell at the top of our lungs that we're pissed off and that we're sick and tired of giving our hearts and souls to people who could care less about anyone but themselves?

When do we forgive ourselves for thinking that we could make a difference?

I am sad to admit that I do not have the answers to these questions, but I'm still here. I'm still teaching and loving and hoping. I still embrace that which I do not recognize as 'right,' and I do what I can. I do what I can, not to change an unwilling soul, but to share the light.

Alan Paton once wrote, "To give up the task of reforming society is to give up one's responsibility as a free man."

So like a survivor of a 20-car pileup, I emerge from the thick smoke and the twisted metal staggering but determined; shaken, but undaunted. I understand the significance of my survival and although I'm still reeling, I get it.

I have been blessed with a strong sense of purpose and a healthy self-esteem, and I have known my entire life that I was put on this earth to affect change. I am here to do what I can.

.-.

Did you know that *a child is abused every seven seconds*? In the time it takes us to put cream and sugar in our coffee, another child has been violated, usually by a member of his or her own family.

Did you know that *every three minutes a child dies from abuse*? How long does it take you to brush your teeth? Think about it next time you're getting ready for work. Pay attention to the fact that by the time you're finished shaving, another innocent child has died at the hands of an adult.

Did you know that *by age 18, one in five girls, and one in seven boys are sexually abused*? Studies say that 90% of these kids know their abusers. Next time you're watching your kids play soccer, look around: one in five. One in seven. Evil feeds on innocence and opportunity.

Did you know that there's something *you* can do? Did you know that you are an agent of change and that your compassion can save someone's life? Go to the final section of this book and see how you can transform the life of someone you know or someone you've never met. I challenge you to stand up for those who cannot stand up for themselves. I challenge you to take yourself to the edge and create change. May you find grace in your endeavors…

> *"The chief problem of any community cursed with crime is not the punishment of the criminals, but the preventing of the young from being trained to commit crime..."*
>
> ~W.E.B. Du Bois

"What do you call it when someone sits there all day and thinks about crazy stuff?" He was 14 years old and a student of mine at the county jail. He had been diagnosed with Bipolar Disorder before he was five.

"I don't know, what do you mean by 'crazy stuff'?" I asked innocently. "YouknowwhatI'msayin', crazy stuff, off 'da chain kind of things, youknowwhatI'msayin'?" Usually I would require that he speak proper English. On a normal day, I would say something like: "how can I know what you're saying if all you're saying is 'youknowwhatI'msayin'?'!" For some reason on that day, I let it go. His expression unnerved me. Perhaps it was because his face was 'expression-*less*.' "Well, I'm not sure what you mean - 'crazy violent,' or just 'crazy stupid'?" "Well," he smirked, all 4 foot 5 inches of him, "kinda 'crazy violent things,' youknowwhatI'msayin'?" I gave him the *'"School Teacher glare,'* a look I had inherited from my mom and had perfected before I taught my first class. Sort of a slow, side-ways glance that says I'm losing patience. He fidgeted and giggled nervously, and although I gave him very little room when it came to these types of discussions, he knew I cared.

His was a sweet smile, a blatant contradiction. This 14 year old boy had been arrested for the 8th time. These particular charges indicated a terrifying escalation in violence: Attempted Murder, Carjacking, Assault with a Deadly Weapon, and Attempted Kidnapping. The latest incident occurred in broad daylight, just a mile or so from his home, at a gas station where a young mother was innocently filling up her SUV. He and his 15 year old home boy had been scoping out the parking lot all day when they decided hers was the 'ride' they wanted. They had been scheming, trying to find a way to get across town to 'hook-up' with their girlfriends, also in their early teens.

So like a lion stalking its' prey, he snuck up behind the unsuspecting woman, put a 6 inch blade to her throat and demanded her keys. With her 8 year old daughter buckled 'safely' in the back seat of her Suburban, this valiant young mother chose not to give in. Frantic, he snatched the keys and pushed her to the ground, then, laughing out loud, howling actually, he began to take off with the girl in the car. He burned rubber and attempted to exit the parking lot, but the desperate mother jumped up and grabbed the door of the moving vehicle. He dragged her across the pavement, screaming and pleading with him to let her daughter go. Smugly, he slammed on the brakes, shoved the car in park and pulled out the 6-inch blade. Cackling, he pointed it at the little girl who was by that point, terrified and sobbing and begging for her mother. While the mom pleaded for her daughter's life, he lunged at the girl with knife, sliced it through the seatbelt strap and threw the child onto the pavement. His buddy jumped into the vehicle and they sped off.

He smiled proudly and informed me that he had 'made her squirm.'

Before they got to their destination, the cops were hot on their tail. While fleeing from the police in the stolen vehicle at speeds exceeding 100 mph, the 14 and 15 year olds were rapturous. Laughing and high fiving each other, the young driver didn't see the stop sign ahead. He could barely see over the steering wheel. Without ever hitting the brakes, he broadsided an elderly couple on their way to a doctor's appointment. He was charged with attempted murder. If the old man, the passenger who took the full force of the impact died, this kid would never see the light of day again.

The other boys in my class knew him well and said he grew up in a small, crowded, filthy trailer in a tiny suburb on the outskirts of a college town in north central Florida. They said he was embarrassed to bring people home. He hated it there himself, so he basically grew up on the streets. His parents seldom knew where he was at any given time. His three older brothers had been in and out of juvenile detention facilities since grade school. They have all done prison time. Two will grow old there.

I ask you this, Ladies and Gentlemen: why is it that the law requires us to obtain a license to drive and hunt and fish but *any*one can breed? For the record: I do not apologize for that question. We all know that not everyone is cut out to be a parent. We all suffer the consequences of what I call non-parenting. Is this a societal problem? Are we, as citizens responsible for preventing such calamities? I believe we are.

If you don't know who your kids are hanging out with, *find out*. If they are coming home at all hours of the night, *put a stop to it*. If they spend hours online on Face Book or in chat rooms, get involved in their lives and *set limits*. **Of course it's a pain in the ass to deal with teenagers – they live on "Planet Me,"** but it's far better than the alternative – that phone call or visit from your local Sheriff in the middle of the night.

Did you know that prescriptions pills have become the new crack cocaine for middle class kids? Are *your* kids experimenting with pills? Would you even know it if they were? Have you checked your medicine cabinet lately?

I believe we have the ability to create positive change in our own homes as well as in our communities. I challenge you to turn off your cell phone, put down the video game, turn off those ridiculous reality shows, leave work a little early just one day a week, and become a mentor – even if it's for your own kid. If your kids are grown or you never had any of your own, there are countless ways to affect change. Whether you believe it or not, you can make a huge difference in the life of a confused teenager on the brink. Become involved in such life-changing agencies as the Guardian AdLitem program or Big Brothers/Big Sisters. Tutor kids at your local school, sit and listen to your niece or nephew or tell a neighbor kid you think they matter. No matter what you think of yourself: 'too fat, too clumsy, too out of shape, too old, too young, too this or too that' – there is a kid out there somewhere who will love you just for showing up - a kid who is waiting for someone just like you to waltz in and save their life.

I think you're perfect for the job.

Godspeed.

> *"Love, compassion and tolerance are necessities, not options. Without them, humanity cannot survive…"*
>
> ~The Dalai Lama

It was a typical day in jail and I was teaching a class of female inmates when I heard Lakeisha, a girl I'd known both inside and outside of the jail for quite a few years, whispering to a new student saying something like: *"go ahead and ask her, Miss Honey, Miss Leanne, she love animals, she'll know what to do!"* "Oh, I don't think I should," Judy (Miss Honey) replied, "I don't want to bother her with all my personal problems." The black girls had nicknamed her 'Miss Honey' because she looked like a character in a children's story book they remembered. She was 50 years old and rail thin with reddish hair and big glasses. She had a dry sense of humor and she made us all laugh.

She was like their mom and they all loved her.

"Ask me what, Judy," I said. "Oh, I don't want to get you into any trouble, I'll figure something out." "I can't do much under the circumstances, but where there are animals

169

involved, I'll definitely do anything I can to help." When you work in the criminal justice system, it is taboo, and borderline illegal, to assist inmates with personal issues. There is a protocol in place and we are strongly advised to respect it, mostly for our own protection.

"Well," she finally said, "I think we live in the same neighborhood because before I came in here I saw you walking a big white dog, and, well, anyway, I've got a few cats - people in the neighborhood used to call me 'The Cat Lady!'," she said giggling nervously. "Well, I'm awful worried about them, but I'm especially concerned about the oldest one." "Where do you live, Jude, and who's taking care of your cats now?" "I live just around the corner from you with my mom. She's 70 years old, but she's in jail too, both of us for DUI, isn't that pathetic?!" "Anyway, right now, there's no one there to look out for my babies and I'm just a wreck about it!" "Well, I can see why, my animals are like my kids too," I said sympathetically, "I'll go check on them after work." "Oh my

God," she said with tears welling up in her eyes, "the girls all said you were an angel."

"So do they have names?" I asked. "Well, yeah," she said lighting up, "there's Chippers, he's got long, black hair, and he's a gentleman, and then there's Little Kitty, she's a pretty little thing with long brown and black hair, and she's so darn sweet, and of course there's Calamari, she's a big fat, fluffy Siamese with beautiful blue eyes. She can be kind of persnickety, but she's a love…" She paused, "that's only three," I said. "Well, then there's the oldest one, she's everybody's mama! She's the one I'm really worried about, but I'd rather not tell you her name," she said sheepishly, "these darn girls will just poke fun!" "Go ahead and tell her, Miss Honey, we won't laugh," Lakeisha said, patting her gently on the shoulder. "Oh come on now, Judy, how can I get her to come to me if I don't know her name?" "Well," she said with her head down and smirking, knowing full well what was coming, "well, Miss Leanne, her name is… Kitty Witty."

"Kitty Witty!!!" Lakeisha squealed, squinting with disbelief, *"what 'da hell kinda name is Kitty Witty?!"* The entire classroom was in hysterics. "See! I told you they'd just poke fun!" The room was alive with laughter, the girls all hugged her and told her it everything would be OK because Miss Leanne loved animals and Miss Leanne would take care of them. They were right.

That afternoon after work, not knowing what to expect, I drove to the vacant house on the corner. It had obviously been neglected for quite some time – windows were broken, plants were dying, the front door was ajar, and some of the furniture was missing. The power had been cut off, the place was dark and eerie, and blankets had been hung over a couple of the windows. Neighbors had whispered that it had turned into a crack house, so I had no desire to see who may be squatting there. I went around to the side and called their names. Like hidden creatures from the forest, they emerged tentatively from their hiding places. They were so thin and so scared, but when I opened a can of cat food, Chippers, Little

Kitty and Calamari seemed to know I wasn't there to harm

them. I fed them and loved on them and scanned the yard for

Kitty Witty.

After a few minutes and no Kitty Witty, I was getting a

little concerned so I trotted to the back yard and lo and behold,

there she was. Like a super-sized Snow Bird on Miami Beach,

she lay there sprawled in the middle of the grass-less lawn, all

25 pounds of Calico madness basking in the Florida sunshine.

"Uh, 'Kitty Witty?'…" I said tentatively, and suddenly without

shame or concern for anything other than her own indulgence,

she jerked around, jumped up, and raised her front paw high in

the air like a Kindergartner on her first day of school - *'HERE!',*

she practically shrieked, *"WHERE IN GOD'S NAME HAVE*

YOU BEEN?! A GIRL COULD STARVE OUT HERE!' She

jumped up and flew across the lawn like a projectile right

through the broken down fence, straight to my car parked on

the side of the road. She rode in the front seat like a diva in a limo, her paws perched on the dash practically commanding my every turn…sort of like a hairy GPS. She fit right into my menagerie of dogs and cats. She actually became like the CEO – not even my 70 pound bulldog crosses her path…

Judy was ecstatic knowing that her beloved animals were being cared for. As she grew more confident and overcame her fear of Math, she passed her GED in less than a month. Consequently however, while she and her mom were imprisoned, their house went into foreclosure, and tragically, less than a week after her mom was released from prison, she died of complications from a lung disorder.   Judy had no income and couldn't keep up with the payments and she lost her childhood home for good.   Then, as if she hadn't suffered enough, Judy lost the only thing she had left. Frankie, her companion of 10 years died of a tragic diving accident on the Santa Fe River. During a family gathering at a local state park, Frankie did a back flip off the limb of a dead tree hanging over the river, something he'd done since he was a kid. This time, he misjudged the distance, hit his head on the limb, broke his neck and drowned right then and there, in front of his family and friends. They found his body downstream hours later.

More than four years later, 'Miss Honey' has endured years of heartache, but like the Phoenix, she always rises and today she holds a management position and is taking college courses. Calamari has been living with a neighbor down the street and is the queen of her domain. Chippers and Little Kitty are still living at the only place they've ever known as home. Dear friends of mine are living in the house and have fallen in love with those two hard-luck cats. Isn't it incredible how much we can learn from the unconditional love of animals? Isn't it awesome how a shared love of all living creatures can bring people together? I believe it's a lesson we can all benefit from, and a message we *must* leave as a legacy for our children. Gandhi once said: "the greatness of a nation and its moral progress can be judged by the way its animals are treated…"

Judy still struggles, but she still checks in now and then, and whenever I get the chance, I tell her how beautiful and positive and intelligent and significant she is in this world.

God Bless you, 'Miss Honey,' may you someday know how your kind heart and gentle humor has impacted even the most hardened of souls, and how gracefully you've influenced the lives of so many, many people.

Kitty Witty

> *"Until he extends his circle of compassion*
> *to include all living things,*
> *man will not himself find peace…"*
>
> ~Albert Schweitzer

"I got to admit, Miss Leanne, I do love it!"

"That's the most excited I've ever seen you, Kenny." I said, "but the truth is, it's a barbaric act and it makes me sick."

'"I know, it gets a bad name in the news but it's big money, Miss Leanne, big money!"

He was in my GED class at the county jail. He was only 16.

"I just don't understand the cruelty. These are loyal, loving, devoted creatures that would do whatever you told them to do, Kenny. How can you watch them suffer?"

"It ain't exactly watchin' them suffer, Miss Leanne. It's watchin' them fight! That's what I'm talkin' 'bout!"

He high-fives his classmate and they both confirmed their excitement by pumping their fists in the air.

177

"Do you think Michael Vick should be punished?"

"Ooh no, Miss Leanne! He only doin' what everybody else is doin'! He just well known, that's why they goin' after him!"

"But Kenny, he and his buddies brutally tortured the losing dogs; isn't that a crime?"

"I got to tell you, Miss Leanne, when we was young, we used to fight dogs out near Payne's Prairie and when they lost, we'd feed them to the gators and they was still alive too, just like Michael Vick's dogs!"

Another high-five followed by enthusiastic nods of approval, both grinning from ear to ear. They had each experienced this barbaric ritual. They acted out the process by forcing a pretend pit bull into the murky swamps of north central Florida: "Go on now, get on in there!"

They mimicked the dog looking back at them with its head down. They described its body shaking and its tail between its legs. They told of the alligators waiting in plain sight just feet away. "Get on in there now!" they repeated, both laughing and feeling smug.

"Does it make you feel powerful because your faithful, loyal dog followed your orders and waded into those dark waters to an unthinkable death?"

They looked confused.

"Dear God," I whispered as I turned my back and began to cry.

"Oh, we're sorry, Miss Leanne! We didn't mean to make you cry! We're really sorry!"

"Don't feel sorry for me; be afraid for yourselves."

As I thought about what I said, I realized that they were only babies – boys who had been forced to grow up far too fast in order to survive. I knew that their laughter was nothing more than a defense mechanism concocted to prove their manliness and stature within their community.

"You need to know that whoever put you through that is sick and abusive and belongs behind bars."

They bowed their heads and apologized again. "Maybe you is right, Miss Leanne, I never thought about it that way."

....

On another day during GED class with a new group of juvenile boys the subject of dog fighting came up yet again. "Why," I blurted out, "does anyone think suffering is acceptable?"

"Because it isn't about the suffering, Miss Leanne," Terrell answered in a more articulate manner than most of his peers. "It's about the sport."

"Sport? How on earth can anyone consider watching animals tear each other apart and fight until the death a sport?"

He had no answer. He had just seen the photos of my English Bulldog Zsa Zsa that I purposefully show to all of my students because I feel it's important for them to experience some sort of connection, an obvious human-animal bond that they rarely experience growing up. I have ridiculous shots of her in a bikini I bought at Wal-Mart, sitting in a corner hiding from the thunder, and loving on my cats – disproving their belief that all dogs hate cats and try to eat them and that bull dogs are born to fight.

He smiled his beautiful smile and related to me how much a person could love their dog – how much he loved *his* dog. He even showed me the tattoo he designed of his favorite dog. "That's sweet, Terrell," I shared.

I wasn't even close to being prepared for what came next.

"When I was six or seven my family had to move because we couldn't afford to stay there anymore. My dad had champion Pit Bulls and didn't want anyone else to have them and he sure didn't want to shoot them."

"So what did he do with them?" I asked not really wanting to know the answer. "He chained them up in the back yard and we left."

"I beg your pardon?"

"Yep, he loaded us all into the car and we moved just like he said we were going to."

My mouth had dropped open and I felt tears burning in my eyes but words would not come.

"About six months later we went back to that place to pick up some things and remember, I was only a little kid so the first thing I did was run out back to see my dogs." "Dear God, Terrell, I'm so sorry."

"Yeah, all I found was the chain still hooked on to the collar that was attached to a skeleton with fur on it. I started to cry and my dad came up behind me and squeezed my shoulder and said, "There ain't no room for tears – act like a man! You got my blood flowin' through your veins so stop actin' like a girl!"

I saw the tears welling up in his big brown eyes and as his smooth, velvety, DJ-like voice began to crack, I changed the subject because the other students were beginning to fidget. They didn't want to see their home boy lose it and I had no desire to hear the rest of the story. After class I called him aside and offered an ear should he need it, but like a man, he said, "I'm over that, Miss Leanne but believe me, my mind has definitely changed about dog fighting." During class a couple of days later I asked the boys what they would do to make this world a better place. I said "aren't you tired of being a part of the problem, gentlemen? Wouldn't it be awesome to be a part of the solution?" Terrell beamed and said," I'd start a rescue and adoption group for Pit Bulls. I'd save them from the savagery and put them in loving homes where they were safe and loved, not starved and beaten. You know something, Miss Leanne, Pit Bulls really are a gentle breed. You gotta work real hard to make 'em mean." Sadly, the other boys couldn't think of anything, in fact, they didn't see themselves as culpable at all. "How can we be part of the problem, Miss Leanne if we is just supplyin' what rich college kids and basers (people who free-base or smoke crack cocaine) want? When you get right down to it, we IS the solution!" "Shit, if we didn't make the money somebody else would."

Because of my job, I have many conversations during which people ask me why I think things are so bad in our society. They know that I have taught in jails and in welfare transition programs for more than 20 years and they know that I have immersed myself in a culture I may never understand because I love my job. I say unapologetically, however, that the innate lack of compassion and a sense of unconditional love for all living things, coupled with the obsession with money and possessions is the core issue.

I say that within the culture of crime and poverty, money and morality simply do not coexist.

- I've seen people sell their children for crack cocaine.
- I've seen people sell drugs to their own addicted mothers, fathers, sisters and brothers just to buy a new set of rims.

- I've seen pre-adolescent girls attack each other for an article of clothing that they felt entitled to have for themselves.

- I've been in the projects and have seen nine-year-old girls fighting viciously, drawing blood over the affections of a fourteen-year-old boy because their mama said they "Gots to protect their man."

- I've seen seven-year-old boys standing point on the street corner learning the business of selling drugs.

- I've seen young mothers wait in line for hours at the county jail, their small children and infants crying and fidgeting and sweating, just so they can spend an hour a week with their 'baby daddy.'

- I've seen many young women with infants and small children waiting to see the *same* 'baby daddy.'

When compassion is not practiced or taught in the home, we as a society must change our paradigm and begin to teach it wherever and whenever we can. When did we stop teaching manners and common courtesy in school? The results are both obvious and frightening. Just look what has happened to our children since the budget for Physical Education disappeared. The responsibility for the moral crisis in which we are mired rests on our own shoulders and we should all take it personally.

Fighting dogs is illegal and monstrous. Believe it or not, you can do something to stop it. First and most importantly, please understand that these dogs are not to blame. An animal is usually only as vicious as we make it, and most Pit Bulls are extremely gentle by nature.

Here are a few suggestions:

- When you see ads in your local paper for dogs or cats that are "Free to a Good Home," call the number and warn that person that this is often where 'bait' comes from. Warn them that their family pet could actually be used to make Pit Bulls mean – that they could be torn to shreds by a vicious fighting dog just for practice and a few laughs.

- There was a recent story in the news that a "kitten mill" had been raided and dozens of cats and kittens were rescued. Not only is it bad enough that people over-breed dogs and cats when there are so many waiting in shelters to be adopted, *but these particular kittens were being bred to be used as Pit Bull bait!*

- Spay and neuter your own animals so their offspring don't end up in shelters where sadistic Pit Bull owners also find their bait.

- Boycott websites and establishments that either support dog fighting or sell "how-to" books or fighting videos.

- Report any known dog fighting activity in your area. There is usually a hefty reward – often thousands of dollars.

- Instead of spending hundreds of dollars on a pure-bred puppy, take a trip to your local shelter. There are so many wonderful, loving creatures that need you.

- Write to your state representative and compel them to get legislation on the books that will make the punishment fit the crime.

- Again, remember that the Pit Bull breed is not the enemy. It is the monsters who make them mean who need to be punished.

You don't have to put your life in danger. A phone call, a letter or a conscious act of compassion toward helpless victims – be they children, the elderly, friends, family or even animals – will truly make a difference.

Life, in *all* forms, matters. Do what you can.

> *"I have learned much from my teachers,*
> *and from my peers, even more than from my teachers;*
> *but from my students, more than from all ..."*
>
> ~The Haggadah

I learned how to make crack cocaine today.

As a teacher in the correctional system, I learn a great deal from my students, and far too often, I see and hear more than I really want to. While sitting in GED class with two of my juvenile students at the county jail, they nonchalantly asked if I knew how easy it was to make crack.

"Now why on earth would I know how to make crack cocaine?!"

"We was just askin', Miss Leanne," they bumped fists and giggled like little boys. Sadly, that's exactly what they were – little boys charged with very grown-up crimes. "Just asking? There's obviously something you want to talk about, so by all means, go right ahead and enlighten me." Without missing a beat, they shared with me the recipe for a 'crack cookie' as it is called. "It's simple, Miss Leanne," they grinned, and explained how to create a pan-sized cookie-like concoction that will later be broken into tiny pieces and sold as 'rock.' Rock is the piece of cocaine that goes into a crack pipe.

"Well you see, Miss Leanne, I only started dealin' drugs so I didn't have to go into Foster Care," Vin said matter-of-factly while in the middle of a Pre-Test.

"What do you mean, Vin?" I asked a bit skeptically.

"They sent my dad to prison for 20 years for dealin', so that left me and my mom, but she was dealin' and usin' too. By the time she went to jail, I was 13 and DCF (Department of Children and Families) said I had to go into the system. I said no way. I done heard about kids like me in foster care: rapes, beatin's. Ain't no way I was gonna be somebody's little bitch." He high-fived his homey sitting next to him.

"Well, how did dealing keep you out of Foster Care?" I was confused but already starting to feel my stomach turn.

"I lived on the streets for about two weeks, sleepin' in parks and doorways, tryin' to stay out of sight, when somebody

asked me if I wanted to make some money, so I started dealin'
so I could eat. When I had a little money, I gave a little down-
payment to a friend and she said I could move in and stay on
her couch as long as I paid rent and helped with groceries. He
spoke like a seasoned veteran as he shared the anguish of his
years on the battlefront. "I seen just about all there is to see,
Miss Leanne."

"I'm sure you have, honey. I'm sorry for that."

Four years later, at 17, Vin was sitting in county jail
awaiting sentencing. He had been arrested for dealing drugs for
the fourth time and would soon learn how long he would have
to share a cell with a convicted criminal in the Florida
Department of Corrections.

"Is your mom clean now, Vin?"

"Yeah, but only 'cause she's still locked up."

"And your dad?"

"I ain't talked to him since I was about nine years old,
but I just got a letter from him. He's still in prison but he sent a

letter to my auntie's house wantin' to know where I was so she sent it here to me. I wasn't sure if I would or not, but I wrote him back." "Have you heard from him again?" "Nope, I shoulda knowed better than to trust him. It's not like I give a shit anyway." He would have dropped dead right then and there before revealing to anyone how much his dad's snub had upset him. Their strength amazes me sometimes.

"*My* dad got sent up for 15 years," Amos chimed in. "I was only 'bout 9 or 10." His mom was deaf and as he talked about how he had been the man of the house and how he had communicated with his mom in sign language since he was two or three, he lit up and the energy in the room had visibly changed. Amos was a very dark-skinned kid with pearl-white teeth in desperate need of braces. I was quite sure he had endured extreme ridicule prior to getting kicked out of school, yet he was surprisingly self-confident. Perhaps it was the $20,000.00 dollars he claimed to have had stashed under his bed because he knew someday he would get caught and need a good lawyer. "I'm a saver, Miss Leanne," Amos said proudly with a huge grin.

"Ooh, not me," Vin blurted out. "I gots to have me a new pair of Timberlands!" They bumped fists and laughed out loud. "I like my outfits now too, Miss Leanne," Vin said grinning.

"Please don't tell me you're one of those guys that struts around in one of those hideous ensembles with matching plaid shorts, shirts and hats!"

"Yep, that's me!" he exclaimed, still grinning. "The girls love a man in a nice suit!"

"A tailored suit maybe, sweetie," I said shaking my head, "not a clown suit!"

The boys looked at each other, shook their heads and laughed out loud.

"So Amos, what do you mean you have $20,000.00 under your bed?"

"Oh, yes, ma'am, soon as I got sent over here from Juvie (the Juvenile Detention facility across the street), I called my mama and told her to take $15,000.00 from the box under my bed. "Go down and give $10,000.00 to the best attorney in town and keep five for yourself."

"So that was drug money?"

"Well, yeah, I didn't know no other way of makin' money, Miss Leanne. I been on the streets tryin' to support me and my mom since I was 10 or 11."

"So, what's wrong with this picture? Both of you guys have family in prison for selling and using?"

"Yeah," they said shrugging their shoulders trying to follow my line of questioning.

"You judge them and you despise them yet you're following in their footsteps." They both looked to the floor and started fidgeting.

"I'm not slamming either one of you here, believe me. I am not a judge nor a jury, please know that, but where does it end?"

Neither had an answer.

"Doesn't either of you feel guilty about selling to someone else's mom, dad, sister, daughter or son?"

"If they got the money, they get what they ask for, Miss Leanne. We ain't here to judge nobody neither. We got bills to pay like everybody else."

"I don't think you follow what I'm saying. Both of your lives have been turned upside down over drugs. What would you do to the guy who turned your baby sister or your mama on to her first hit of crack?"

"I'd kill the motherfucker!" Vin shouted.

"Oh, yeah, I'd put a bullet in him right quick," Amos agreed.

"So you have no problem selling that first hit to someone *else's* baby sister or mom?"

The silence was palpable. They would chew on that one for some time but I knew it wouldn't change a thing. How could I expect it to? Did I really expect these boys to have an answer? There's a fine line between morality and survival – these boys walk that tight rope 24/7. God help them.

My job as a teacher under these circumstances is to provide the best free and public education possible while doing my best to understand and accept the culture into which I have immersed myself. The most golden opportunities present themselves when we open our minds and initiate honest dialogue without judgment or malice. There are days when I am completely and blatantly overwhelmed and deeply frustrated by how helpless and naïve I really am. When I take the opportunity to step outside my own reality and absorb the true nature of my chosen profession in my chosen surroundings, I am humbled and grateful to know that every day I have an opportunity to affect change on this earth. That change may not be immediately evident, but somewhere under some hideous circumstances, my words may ring true and someone may make a different choice.

We live and hope.

Do the Crime…

Do the crime, do the time-
…How you gonna try me like that?
Nothin' to gain when you're off 'da chain-
…How you gonna try me like that?
'Three strikes and I'm out' –man, what's that shit about?
…How you gonna try me like that?
Bitch say she cry every night-say she sick of the fight-
…How you gonna try me like that?
She say we ain't got no heat-baby need shoes on his feet-
How you gonna try me like that?
Three hots and a cot - Yo, bitch! dat's all I got-
…How you gonna try me like that?
Yo, somebody said some towers fell –
fuck, I already be livin' in hell-
…How you gonna try me like that?
Somebody said we got to unite and
come together and put up a fight.
Well, who 'da fuck's gonna fight for me-
and show me a little liberty?
'Cuz all I see is supply and demand-
the rich man slaps some cash in my hand-
I give him the shit and then I get him some more-
tell me this ain't no fuckin' war…
How you gonna try me like that?
I say how you gonna try me like that?

I wrote this poem for Mike. in the fall of 2001 just after the 9.11 attacks. He loved it. Mike was one of my juvenile GED students at the county jail. Obviously one of his favorite things to say was "How you gonna try me like that?" In proper English, to "try" someone is to give them a hard time, to challenge them. He would say this to me just to get a reaction. I made sure he always got one. He was smart, incredibly serious and often morose, but his smile could light up a room. He was a victim of his own culture.

He began running the streets and dealing drugs when he was ten. Seven years later, and after countless attempts by the state to 'rehabilitate' him, he was looking at ten-to-fifteen years in prison. He was still a boy.

Through my teaching and my writing, it is my desire to shed new light on a culture many of us will never understand, and to give the benefit of the doubt when it seems as though the answer is cut and dry. When we open our hearts, strength and inspiration reveal themselves in peculiar ways.

I work in a system that does not keep its promises. I work with children who are forced to become adults far too soon because their role models are turning tricks, free-basing crack cocaine in front of them, and standing on street corners killing their own people. They blame their weaknesses on their addictions and their addictions on their weaknesses. They excuse their behavior in the name of poverty and pray for forgiveness in the name of God. The answers become questions and the questions have no answers. How did we get here? How will we survive? Will you light a candle or curse the darkness? It matters.

*November 6, 2012:

As I was scrolling through the inmate population log seeking candidates for the next GED exam, I came across a familiar name. Mike Curry was back. More than a decade later, I wondered if he would remember me or the poem I wrote for him. Would he remember the days in class with Larry and Eric? Would he shake my hand and smile that electric smile, or had he been hardened and tainted by the system? I would never know unless I reached out, so I did. I printed out this chapter, wrote "Light your candle, Mike," signed the bottom of the page, and made my way to C-Pod, a housing unit for medium and maximum-security inmates in the back of the jail. With the story in hand, I asked one of the officers if I could see him. The guy didn't ask any questions, just yelled "Curry" and went about his business. I would have known him anywhere. He was taken aback at first, and I waited for him to get his bearings. "Hey Mike," I said smiling, "remember me?" "Miss Leanne?!" "You got it, how've you been?" "Wow! You really messed me up! I mean in a good way!" He *did* smile that electric smile – there were a few gold teeth in the front this time, but it was still a beautiful smile and he had a hard time containing his joy.

"I didn't know if you'd remember this poem, but I've written a book and you're a part of it. I wanted you to have a copy of the chapter since it was you who inspired me to write it." "Oh, man!," he said searching for the right words, "I DO remember the poem! I kept it until I went to DOC" (Department of Corrections/prison). "I can't believe you remember *me!*" "Of course I do, those were simpler times, weren't they? Hard to believe it was twelve years ago that you and Larry and Little E and I sat in that classroom. We learned a lot about life and about each other, didn't we?" "Oh, yes ma'am," he said beaming, caressing the papers I had given him as if he was holding on to the Holy Grail. "Did you ever get your GED, sweetie?" "I tried while I was locked up, but they said my scores weren't high enough to take it. Are you still teaching on the outs?" (outside the jail). "Nope, I'm here all day, but if you need a hand when you get out, you know where I am." Again, he beamed. "I'm due out in a few months, Miss Leanne. Can I get in touch with you?" "Of course you can. I look forward to it, Mike."

As he shook my hand, he held on tight and in his eyes I saw a spark, a glimmer of hope that spoke volumes. "Thank you, Miss Leanne," he said softly, looking long into my eyes.

"Thank you so much…"

The way I see it, we must do our best to shine a light in the darkest of places. Making excuses for not acting is not an option. How else can we expect things to change?

> *"He has honor if he holds himself to an ideal of conduct though it is inconvenient, unprofitable or dangerous to do so."*
>
> ~Walter Lippman

It is an unwritten, unspoken code of the streets. Most of us will never, ever understand it, much less agree with it, but as I have come to learn, it is not for us to judge. It is a time-honored standard that is deeply rooted in the hearts, the minds and the souls of many of my students. And although I am troubled by its implications, I recognize the foundation on which it stands. It is about commitment and honoring one's word. It's about never being a snitch.

During my juvenile GED class at the jail I was surrounded by 16 and 17-year-old boys who had committed serious, life-altering adult crimes. We were talking about an unsolved rape in the area and I said I couldn't understand why this guy hadn't been caught.

"This was a brutal, vicious attack on an innocent woman and it happened at 6:00 a.m. in broad daylight while she was jogging less than 100 yards from her house. Why on earth can't someone identify this monster?" I said looking around the room.

"I know who he is," one of my boys whispered proudly. He kept on working, but looked up slightly from the page to check my reaction.

"Really?" I asked a bit skeptically.

"Yep," he said gloating. The tension began to seep into the room like a foul odor and the other students started shifting in their seats.

"Well, have you done anything about it?"

"You mean report it or somethin'?"

"Uh, yeah, the woman was violently raped, pistol whipped, violently raped again and left for dead!"

"It's not my business, noaimsayin'?"

"No, I don't know what you're saying. A young mother was jogging right down the street from her house when some sick bastard jumped out of his car, raped her and beat her until she lost consciousness, and then raped her again. She spent weeks in the hospital fighting for her life. How can you say it's none of your business?"

"She wasn't none of my people, noaimsayin'?"

"No, dammit, I don't understand this at all!"

He looked at me a bit confused and when he saw the tears well up in my eyes, he sat up and tried his best to explain the basis of his decision.

"You see, Miss Leanne, I hate the po-lice. My daddy, my uncles, my brothers, everybody I know hates the po-lice. I don't hate the people, noaimsayin'? Just the position, so we handle things in our own way."

"What if she was your sister?"

"Then I'd handle it. Me and my brothers, we'd take care of it and the po-lice don't got to be involved."

"Do you have kids?" I asked.

"Yes I do, and…."

"Boy or a girl?!"

"I got a little girl, but you see, Miss Leanne, I know where you're goin' with this, noaimsayin', but I can't think like that."

"Can't think like what? Can you imagine someone doing what he did to that poor woman to your own innocent daughter?"

"No ma'am," he said, softening for the first time, "no ma'am, I can't. That's why I feel a little different about this one, but I can't break the code, noaimsayin'?"

As I listened in disbelief and held back my emotions, I felt a strange sense of acceptance come over me.

"You know I hate everything you just said and I don't agree with any of it, and I'll probably never forgive you, but I get it and I honor it."

He sat straight up in his chair and looked me dead in the eye, "thank you," he said softly. "Thank you for that, Miss Leanne."

Of course I had to report this to the detectives at the jail and they got nothing out of him. We all knew they wouldn't. They, too, knew the code.

I wrote this story that night. I told him about it and asked him if he'd like to read it. "I didn't mention yours, or any names," I confirmed, "but I think it's only fair that you experience the impact you had on me yesterday." He was visibly moved, and after reading this particular account, he asked if he could read the rest of my stories. He devoured them. Every time I see him, in or outside of the jail he asks, "Miss Leanne, is your book out yet? I need to get a copy! That was some powerful stuff!"

"I'll let you know, sweetie. I'll dedicate this chapter to you."

He grinned and hugged me, tentatively at first, but then let go, like he was hugging his mama or his grandma. I felt him shaking.

I often tell my students that I believe hypocrisy is the eighth Deadly Sin. I believe that we must have faith in our principles and defend our convictions with courage and integrity. Two days later I told this story in my GED class at the Job Corps center just down the street. The six boys who sat in my class that morning got it. They all knew the code and they followed it like Marines.

"Those boys got it straight, Miss Leanne. We take care of our own business. That's how it's always been done."

"I seen beatins, shootins, stabbins. I ain't gonna say nothin'."

"When does it end?" I asked.

"When does what end?"

"The killing of the killer of the killer," I spouted. "This is not the Wild Wild West - we have laws for a reason! What if this guy did that to your sister or your mama?" "We'd hunt him down and see to it, that's what!" They high-fived each other and wondered aloud why I was frustrated.

"All right," I said with all the drama I could muster. "What if it was me?"

They froze.

"I'm not your kin, but could you turn away? Could you have this same sense of righteousness if it had happened to me?"

"Oh, now, that's not fair, Miss Leanne! You *is* like family."

I waited.

"Well, I'd come up here from south Florida and handle it, that's what!" one of them blurted out.

"Oh, yeah, they ain't no question 'bout takin' care of business, Miss Leanne, but we'd have to do a little research," he said with a wink.

"What makes you think the code is weaker here than in *your* neighborhood? Why would anyone talk to *you*?"

"We got ways, Miss Leanne, we got ways." Two degrees of separation redefined.

How do we, as a civilized, law-abiding society digest this information? What is the answer to such behavior? I say it's dialogue.

Eric Holder, our nation's first black Attorney General, said in a recent interview that America is a "nation of cowards" when it comes to discussing the racial divide. Good for him. I think he's right. Bill Cosby has stepped up and been completely honest about his take on the current state of the African American community. Both have been attacked for their lack of political correctness (PC). Rubbish, I say. Let's get it out there and let's figure out how to stop the bleeding. We can no longer sweep it under the rug and pretend that building more prisons will solve the problem.

I believe we must begin the process by introducing compassion in pre-school. My students in jail and Job Corps tell me that by the time a kid is six or seven, it's too late. I believe that we've lowered the bar and that we have lost track of the importance of common courtesy, good manners, and respect. If decency is not being taught at home – if the role models for our future leaders are free-basing crack cocaine and putting their kids on the streets to sell it, or prostituting themselves to support their habit, or are simply not giving their kids the tools they need and the inspiration they deserve, we must create a curriculum that does just that. Period. How's that for PC?

I'm in. How about you?

213

She's somebody's little girl.

She's somebody's mom.

She's somebody's baby sister.

She's somebody's favorite aunt. She's somebody's best friend.

She's an addict. She's a prostitute. She's a victim.

She's two out of three female students in my GED class at the county jail.

As a society, we have failed these women. We should be ashamed of ourselves, yet we judge them. We should be thankful that she is not *our* child, yet we should pray to God *every single night* that our own daughters never take that first hit, swallow that first pill or meet that one charming guy who promises her the moon then beats her to a bloody pulp just to prove she belongs to him. I worry about them like they're my own. Only when they are re-arrested and sent back to jail do I know they are alive. My heart sinks and sings at the same time as I see them marching past my door on the way to their cell. They bow their heads in shame but know that I judge them not. I have no idea how they keep going…

My friends, we should build our little girls up *every chance we get.* We should tell them every single day that they are brilliant and beautiful and capable and talented and significant. We NEED to tell them that they do not need a man, or a woman to justify their existence, that the most vital and profound relationship they will ever have is with themselves.

Did your parents tell you those things? Mine did and I am grateful to them every day of my life.

These are the stories of little girls lost. Please keep them in your prayers.

Cassidy

She was born the youngest of three girls into a prominent local family. She was the apple of her daddy's eye. She worked on the family farm with her grandparents and followed her big sisters everywhere they went. She was adorable and smart and curious. She loved school and had lots of friends. She ran away from home at 16 because she felt constrained by her parents' rules. Her life would *never* be the same...

After hitch hiking the 8 mile ride to the city, she was "befriended" by a group of men at a downtown park, a place frequented by the homeless and rife with drug activity. They seemed kind and promised to care for her like she was their own daughter. She was relieved and thanked them for protecting her.

Before she knew what was happening, they had lured her to a local crack house where she was raped repeatedly by the very men who had promised to watch over her. They introduced her to crack cocaine and held against her will in a hell-hole for nearly three weeks. Her face would end up on a milk carton and her family would be despondent over her disappearance.

I met Cassidy when she enrolled in my GED class at the jail. She was relaxed and intelligent. She tutored and mentored the other students and although she put them at ease, she had a sense of arrogance about her, like she had earned her stripes or something. She, like most of my female students, put up a rugged exterior to mask the pain and shame, but inside these walls I see the very core of their being. She was indeed a little girl who missed her daddy and prayed that her mom would forgive her one more time. She claimed she could never go home again and that she could care less if they answered her calls. She claimed she was happy being surrounded by "real friends, girls in the same predicament, and dope boys who claimed they cared about her and had her back." She worked hard and passed the GED with flying colors.

During class one day, she asked if she could share a story with us in hopes of deterring the younger girls from choosing the same path. "Of course," I chirped. These are great teaching moments. When she was finished reading what she had written, I was no longer chirping. She shared with the class a typical day on the streets – to you and me, not so typical. Utterly unfathomable…Here is her story:

"...as soon as I got out of one tricks' car, another trick was stopping to pick me up – until soon, I got into the wrong car. [It was] a newer white 4-door with a paper tag in the window. When I got in, I smiled, he smiled and we were off to find a secluded area. After finding a secluded area, he suggested we get out of the car to have sex. After getting out of the car and moving to the back where the trunk was is the last thing I remember. When I woke up, I was in a little room built out of ply-wood. I was naked and lying on a mat covered in blood – my blood and maybe someone else's blood that was there before me. I remember my head pounding so bad I thought I had drums inside my brain. I reached up and touched the back of my head and felt a knot and two puncture wounds. Then I began to think, 'will I live or will I die?' Shortly after that I got enough strength and courage and tried to escape. I *was not successful. Now I'm screaming. Screaming and hoping someone will hear my cry for help and rescue me. But the only person who heard my screams was my predator. He opened the door, rushed in at me and told me to shut the fuck up or he would kill me. I stopped screaming but I could not stop crying. Then he told me to lay face down on the mat. I was once told that the worst thing you can do is fight your rapist, so I did as I was told and let him have his way with me. He raped me anally, vaginally and made me perform oral sex on him. This went on for three days. During that time, I was raped so many times I lost count. Thoughts of my family, friends and other loved ones ran through my mind. 'Will I live to see them again or will I die?' By the third day, I was so hungry and thirsty and scared that I was delusional. I was weak and had given up on all hope of making it out of there alive that I was ready to die so that the misery would end. Sometime during that third day, close to nightfall, my predator opened the door and stepped in with a neck tie. I thought he* was going to strangle me to death. Instead, he told me to tie the neck tie around my eyes. So I did as I was told. Then he told me he was putting me in the trunk of his car. 'When I pop the trunk, you can get out.' I thought he was lying. So then I asked him if I could have some clothes. He replied with – 'clothes bitch?! I'm letting you live!' He then grabbed me by the arm, snatched me up and led me to the trunk of the car where I climbed in and he slammed it shut. Immediately I removed the neck tie from my eyes and the car cranked up. For the next twenty to thirty minutes I could hear nothing but the roar of the tires on the highway. I thought he was taking me further into some woods to kill me and dump my body. Then I began to hear sounds of the city. Not even ten minutes later, he yelled at me- get ready to get out, bitch!' The trunk popped and the car stopped for maybe a second. I tried to get out so fast I fell and hit the pavement outside the entrance to the food court at the mall. I was in such shock I couldn't even move. A man came running from the parking lot once he seen me and *gave me his long t-shirt to cover my naked body. He waited*

with me until the cops and the ambulance got there. I was

taken to the hospital where the doctors did a rape kit on me and

determined that I was hit in the back of the head with the claw

part of a hammer. I was treated with lots of care and concern

by the doctors and nurses and the police. I was even referred

to the Health Department for rape victim classes.

Unfortunately, I never went to those classes.

I went back to the streets. Most people think addicts use drugs

to feel good, but I use drugs so I don't have to feel at all. A

thought that crosses my mind sometimes is that my predator

was never caught. He is still out there and probably will never

be caught..."

Today, more than 15 years after she ran away from

home, Cassidy is still in and out of jail, still smoking crack and

still turning tricks. She has tried rehab many times but couldn't

live by the rules. She has been estranged from her family for

years and has no contact with any of them. They've been

through hell worrying about her, bailing her out of jail, and visiting her in rehab, but there comes a time when your child is no longer your baby; a time when the delightful little girl who used to wake up singing is gone. I have spoken with her family and they miss their daughter. They missed her prom, her graduation, and her wedding. They will never know the joy of being grandparents. Her dad is heartbroken and cries when he speaks of her. They have no hope left and without hope, from where does our strength come? I wish I knew…

"Kayla"

At the age of 23, she looked to be 13 or 14 years old, like a cherub with chubby cheeks and the sweetest smile. She was highly intelligent and eager to please. She had been diagnosed with ADHD as a child and was easily distracted. When she could no longer concentrate in class, she would stand on a table with a huge wad of soaked paper towels and clean my chalk boards. She called herself "Pet," claiming she was the Teacher's Pet. I truly enjoyed her and was admittedly taken aback by her innocence.

For her 15th birthday, her father turned her on to crack cocaine then had sex with her. After he was finished, he shared her with his drunken, doped-up buddies. Nearly nine years later, she has four children, all of whom are in foster care or with various family members. The youngest one was born less than an hour after she finished turning a trick behind a dumpster, and less than 30 minutes after her last hit of crack. Grinning and scanning the room for approval, she proudly shared this fact with the class as if she was reporting on the weather. I felt ill. I was disgusted with the whole lifestyle and sickened by anyone who would have sex with a woman (who looked twelve) in broad daylight behind a dumpster while she was obviously pregnant. I was sorry that she had no idea how beautiful and smart and enchanting she was. I had nightmares about her living on the streets. My heart ached for her children who would never know their mother. After she left the county jail, she was sent to prison for a year. She was released from prison nine months later and no one has seen her since.

Angel

"I got OCD, ADHD, SLD, and a whole buncha alphabet behind *my* name, Miss Leanne! My ma says I'm just plain crazy - prob'ly am!" she giggled and shrugged her shoulders as she cleaned the black board and paced all over the room while she rattled off the laundry list of afflictions she claimed to have been born with. At 31 years old, she was tall and lanky and delightful. She was extremely intelligent and awfully fidgety. She was one of the kindest souls I had ever encountered. "Miss Leanne, we gotta fix those maps on the wall," she squealed, "they ain't hung right and they're crooked! You know I can't concentrate if something ain't just right!" "Do what you've got to do, my dear," I said as she had already started another project, stopped to help a fellow student with her essay, and answered another question on her own Pre-GED test. Angel was released before she had a chance to take the actual exam at the jail. She promised me she would take it "on the outs" (outside) and that she would get the financial aid forms filled out for community college and that she would keep in touch. I would never hear from her again.

Just weeks after her release, she was back on the streets. Out there, people look out for one another and everyone loved Angel. Other students have told me that no matter how much or how little she had, she always shared with those who had nothing. She was everyone's best friend and confidant and no matter what, she always found the good in others.

In the wee hours of the morning of June 26th, 2011, Angel was brutally raped and murdered, her battered body dumped in the hedges behind a busy downtown plaza. Those of us who knew her will feel her loss forever.

Do these women really matter? Why should we feel sorry for them if they choose to continue to do drugs and turn tricks? Is addiction a choice? I could rattle off statistics and quote medical professionals, but I'd rather hit you in the gut with stories like these. I'd rather you understood the human side of addiction and pain and loss.

I brought this story up in my juvenile GED class one day and asked the three teenage boys why her death mattered. Two of the three shrugged their shoulders while the other said it mattered because she was someone's daughter. "Yes!" I said looking intently at the other two, "she was somebody's daughter, mother, sister, aunt and friend." Still nothing. Their faces were expressionless. "Where do you draw the line, gentlemen?" "What line, Miss Leanne?" They were puzzled but sitting up a little straighter in their chairs. "The line between what is easy and what is right." "Ooh, wait a minute, Miss Leanne, what we do ain't easy!" I purposely ignored their plea, "the endless quest for money at any cost, the incessant need to buy more stuff with dirty money has turned you and your family and friends into monsters and I happen to know that deep down, you're good boys and you would do anything for your own family, why doesn't someone else's family matter?

What if she had been your mom or your daughter all doped up and on the streets, would you care then?" "Oh, yes ma'am! I'd take care of that right quick!" "But that's my point, honey – she *was* somebody's mom and she was somebody's daughter. Why can't you guys see that drugs ruin countless lives and for what? *The dealer is the problem, the user is the victim.* Chew on that for a minute, boys." They were sixteen and seventeen year old children and they still didn't see the dilemma, so I pressed on. "If you were to face God himself on this day and he said to you: '***my son, have you been part of the problem or part of the solution?***' what would you tell Him?"

"I'd say people is gonna buy drugs from somebody, why shouldn't I be the one to get the money?"

"Unbelievable," I whispered shaking my head, "unbelievable."

I dedicate this story in loving memory of Angel Harris. I wish each and every one of could have experienced the blessing of knowing her.

The following words were written by female inmates while in

GED class. I felt it important to share their voices with you….

My Addiction   Oct 21, 09

I am running, Scared as can be from you; You
Tormented me, Caused me to loose; Caused me
to fall, Your my Addiction. I want you to
leave, but you have me by the tail. Addiction
is a sick disease that lingers in ones Soul day
and night, I am trying to take this fight.
Addiction has you to think it is cool and
Safe, bunch of lies, just to hurt you inside.
Addiction Causes you not to care who you
hurt, and you have to do all Kinds of things
for the next fix. It causes you to endanger your
life, has you in and out of Prision, and jail,
and causes Death. Life is way better than
that, So leave please do, There is a better
world than hurting the ones that cares,
there is God, family and friends.
        I am running Now for the goal
     To Survive, and Stay alive. So Addiction
I do not want you to have Control over
               me;
  Can't you See.

By the Grace of God this I pray, Addiction
to leave my body today

My Bitter Sweet Nightmare

I wake up to face what another day holds, I wrote to you my Story untold. Shower, make-up, money makin gear, Its time for a fix so I'm outta here, I hit the streets, purse full of protection, Making sure my clients are satisfied to perfection. As soon as the money touches my hand, it is quickly removed by my right hand man. This man, he keeps me high, cause God forbid the money run dry. There are days you can pay me to use no rubber, even though in my heart I know there have been others. I try to do everything right, praying to God he dont start another fight. My problem it brings me in + out of jail, I'm secretly praying HIV does not reveal. Men + money will come and go will I make it through another night, only the Good Lord knows. I've been raped, robbed, beat, cut; Still one hit just isn't enough. Cris's voice keeps playing in my head "He's gonna Kill you if you keep going back" But he has what I need the infamous crack. Everyone tries to help and tell me what to do, If they could only imagine half of what I've been through. Getting high helps me become numb, that way when someone says victim I'm no longer the one. So the question + answer you seek "will I relapse? will it all be the Same?" All that's guarantee is if I dont stop my life is what the streets will claim's To be Continued . . . . .

Reliving the Horror

It goes through my mind constantly when my life had turned upside down. I heard this sweet little voice as I put her to bed one night, "___, David has touched me." She was 5 yrs old. I was devestated, lost and out of my mind. I had stayed that way for 8 yrs on the run to drugs Crack-Cocaine to hide the voice that was planted in my head, Not thinking what Crack-Cocaine was adding more horror and misery to my life. Crack-Cocaine had me so messed up in my head, I was out there prosituting. I went to the doctor one day found out I have H.I.V. Down the road to destruction even more. I was adding all this stuff in my life as I go, the child, the doctor, now I run from 2 men that ra,ped me Scared for my life. Instead of the little voice of the child, it's the ra,pist I do, "Get down don't move". I lay here and relive each event that is planted in my mind, the child, the rape and H.I.V 'O' My. I was out on the streets with no care of my life, desperate to find away out of these torments. Some days I would be so out of it, I was hurting others because I felt what the hell I am dying anyways and no one cares, But now I find Someone do. As times

go bye I am afraid and ashamed of knowing
that I could ruined Someones life, I truly
do not know how I can forgive myself for that.
There are some much in my life that is overwhelming.
I am trying to accept that I do have an addiction,
and out of control. Drugs and H.I.V I would not
wish on no one. Every 3 months I go and get my
blood drawn, I watch them fill 6 tubes it is a
reminder of what I have, Painful memories to me,
or my family be like don't go into the kitchen
I will cook the food for you, or bleach the tub
ETC.. I know my life can be better with
determination and the will to do, as long as I
know and tell myself the horror that I lived
I could of prevented most of it by not being out
there. I am an addict with H.I.V. and a life
of pain. An addict that I know I can stop
and better myself. There is always some one
else out there with worst problems than me.
Taking a stand now can save my life, with
God on my side.

The devil stopped by my house one day

The Devil stopped by my house one day
He said he was in a rush and could not stay
I asked the Devil what brings you by
Not too much I just have something I want you to try.
Oh Devil your so great
But little did I know he was using me as bait
That's when the devil pulled the monster from his pocket
Said wanna get high and fly like a rocket
Hell yea I been sad and blue
I could really go for a bump or two
This devil said this isn't cocaine
That for rookies hunny plus its really lame
He said the foil was a boat
One hit from this will make you float
I told the devil I wasn't sure
What I should have done was showed him the door
The devil said it's not that bad
Remember you were feeling sad
This is what my friends do when there feeling blue
All you need is a hit or two
I put the straw up to my lips
One little hit and my lungs filled up quick
As I let the smoke clear from my lungs
I closed my eyes and knew I had just spun
With a smile the devil said
I knew you'd like it yes indeed
Some call it crank some call it speed
I couldn't believe what I had done
He tricked me that devil he said it was fun
Then the devil started for the door
Hey you call me kid, when you want more
Now I gotta go, but don't be mad
On your table I left you a bag

The devil said there was no price
But little did I know I paid with my life
The next day I finished my bag
Then I was back to feeling sad
I remembered what the devils friends did when they were blue
I had his number I knew what to do
I called the devil to see what he'd say
And before I knew it he was on his way
I knew what I was doing was wrong
But I didn't care I just wanted to belong
The devil came back to my house that day
Said he was in a hurry and could not stay
The devil said just so you know it was a trick
I knew when you finished your bag you would be sick
He laughed at me and said your mine
Maybe not this second but give it some time
The devil said to me your life is just a game
And just like the others the monster will affect you the same
And soon I will have your life savings
Just so you can fix your nasty cravings
Oh devil I thought you was my friend
Thick and thin until the end
Oh no you know how I do
I get what I want
And I just used you

Candace Allen

> *"Everybody, my friend, everybody lives*
> *for something better to come.*
> *That's why we want to be considerate of every man –*
> *who knows what's in him, why he was born*
> *and what he can do?"*
>
> ~Maxim Gorky

I got the call just a few days before Christmas. I was in my car on my way out of town and I was helpless.

"Miss Leanne, I wanted you to know I'm okay, but I got caught in the cross fire of some dumb conflict here and got kicked out of my program."

Donna was in a residential drug treatment facility trying desperately to conquer a habit that had held her hostage nearly half her life. She was addicted to crack cocaine. She was only 23. A week earlier while she was in rehab, I had surprised her with a visit and as always, she was appreciative and humbled. She had lived an incredibly difficult life and didn't feel worthy of kindness in any form. She jumped up and down and squealed with delight as I stood rather awkwardly in the lobby holding a poinsettia plant I had bought to spruce up her room. "Hey y'all, this is my teacher!" she broadcast down the hallway. "Can you believe she came to visit *me?*"

She hugged me hard, like a long lost friend and then grabbed my arm and dragged me through the corridors like a favorite Teddy Bear showing me off to anyone in her path.

I had known Donna for about six or seven years. She'd been in my GED class both in jail and in various programs throughout the community. She was bubbly and likeable, hyperactive and sweet. Knowing now what she had been through and she did to survive day to day, it is unfathomable to me how she was *any* of those things. Donna prostituted herself to support her crack habit. She often spoke nonchalantly of her lifestyle as if I could relate to the disgusting men who made her do disgusting things for a few bucks or a rock of cocaine. A few months prior to her arrest, she had been smoking crack with a bunch of people when some guys asked her if she wanted to go for a ride. On a dark, secluded dirt road, this adorable strawberry blonde mother of four was gang-raped and beaten within inches of her life. They threw her bloody, broken body out of the car like trash and dumped her in the middle of the road, in the middle of nowhere, in the middle of the night. She spent the night unconscious and bleeding on the cold dark road and was picked up by a Good Samaritan the next day.

After being asked to leave the treatment program, Donna had nowhere to go. Normally I would have picked her up and offered her a couch, but I was out of town for the holiday. So for three nights during a horrible cold snap, she curled up on the sidewalk outside the homeless shelter because *inside* were old "friends" of hers, old crack buddies, dealers and pimps, all of whom wanted her business back.

Think about it. You're a crack dealer and you have your "regulars," pitiful addicts who need at least $500.00 worth of crack per day to satiate their needs. Say you have ten or twenty or maybe even thirty "clients." That's not a bad "salary" and it's a cash-only business. Needless to say, they'll do whatever they can to keep someone high. Talk about 'freak-enomics.'

So miraculously, Donna steered clear of the demons of her past and kept attending AA and NA meetings and hunted fiercely for a job – any job. She got one at a local restaurant and they have already rewarded her for her initiative and work ethic by giving her a full-time schedule with benefits soon to follow. Her greatest goal was to get her nine- year-old daughter, Julana back. She had three other children, all of whom had been adopted by loving families. She gets to see them often and handles herself with grace.

In this particular child custody case regarding Julana, Donna's parental rights had been terminated. She was allowed to visit Julana at her grandmother's house, but because of her addiction and lifestyle, she had lost her privileges as a mother. She was determined and headstrong and decided that she would do whatever she had to do to restore her parental rights and give Julana the life she herself never had. She wrote a long letter to the judge and begged for another chance. She told him that this time was truly different. She spoke at length of her support groups and sponsors. She told him about her job and her new home. She provided him with references (my name included) and asked that he please call each and every one. Call us he did and I am still stunned by the fact that he granted her a new hearing and a second chance.

I have been a *Guardian AdLitem* (a volunteer legal advocate for children who have been abused, neglected or abandoned), for more than ten years and I have *never* seen this happen. This judge was so impressed with Donna's courage and tenacity that he admitted he couldn't turn her down.

"No one who loses their parental rights goes through this much red tape," he said during our phone conversation. "Most of them just go back out on the streets and have more kids!" he said with disgust. "I agree, Your Honor," I offered. "This is an exceptional case involving an exceptional young woman. Thank you for recognizing that." So in an unprecedented move, he overturned the Termination of her rights and ordered Julana back into her custody. They were both elated.

When Donna was asked to leave the residential program, her counselors realized the conflict wasn't her fault and they recognized her true desire to get clean, so they pulled some strings and got her the first available residence. She was given the keys to a two- bedroom apartment in the projects Mind you, this wasn't a gated community by any stretch of the imagination; in fact, I saw people dealing drugs in the parking lot when I helped move her in, but she was so proud and so appreciative and absolutely delighted with her own place. She couldn't wait to fix up her daughter's room and ready her kitchen for their first meal.

As usual, I went through my cupboards for canned goods, and rooted through closets searching for stuff I hadn't used in a while and passed them on to her. Much like the Buddhists, I see money and material things as energy. Use them for the greater good and Karma takes care of the rest. As

Donna was settling in, the counselors informed her that they often provide recovering addicts with roommates who are experiencing similar challenges. They said that she was doing so well that they considered her a role model and thought she could be a positive influence. Unfortunately, the girl they placed with her wasn't truly ready for change. As they so often do, the roommate ended up relapsing, taking to the streets, smoking crack and then selling her body for more. She was gone for days.

Donna was worried sick because she knew all too well that the fine line between staying clean and slipping off the wagon is often blurred by a lethal combination of addiction and low self-esteem. She was immediately moved into a duplex in a better neighborhood and she was on cloud nine. I got a call at 7:00 a.m. the next morning.

"Miss Leanne, I got my own house! And can you believe it? It's got a backyard with a fence and everything!

Julana can ride her bike down the street without me worryin'! I can't wait to have you over for dinner, Miss Leanne!"

Donna is continuing to pursue her high school diploma and glows when she talks about going to GED class on the campus of a local college: "Miss Leanne, just being able to walk around that campus with people, *healthy* people my own age, all carrying backpacks and studying and planning for their future, Miss Leanne, this is Heaven to me!"

I've decided to save this particular story for last because after sticking with me throughout this entire emotional and often frustrating journey, I get to share with you an honest-to-goodness happy ending. It's been six months and Donna is still clean, still working, still in school, still full of life and yes, she got her daughter back. God bless you, Donna. You're an inspiration to us all.

*I'm sorry to say there is a bittersweet postscript to this particular story. It seems that crack cocaine, like a forbidden lover, has a much stronger lure than even the deep and unconditional bond between a mother and her child. Donna relapsed and went back to the streets. Julana was placed back into the custody of Donna's mom. She wasn't out there long before she was arrested again and placed in jail. She worked hard to get into the Work Release program where inmates are allowed to leave the facility to go to work each day. This is a wonderful, albeit tempting situation for someone in Donna situation, but she's making the most of it. She likes her job, is good at it and the bosses love her. Julana still lives with Donna's mom and Donna sees her daily.

As for me, I'll be right here if the phone rings a next time, and I'll do whatever I can to help her get back on her feet.

My friends, we *all* need someone to answer the call when we're lost. If you or someone you love is battling addiction, or abuse, or demons in any form, please remember this:

"What lies behind us and what lies before us are minor matters compared to what lies within us…"

~Ralph Waldo Emerson

*June, 2012: After more than 12 years of hard work and sheer determination, Donna passed her GED. She bought a cap and gown and walked across the stage with the other graduates – Julana and her family cheering from the stands. She is clean and sober and in a happy and healthy relationship. She plans to attend cosmetology school and she's cleaning houses to get there. She shares a house with Julana and her aunt sand as a hard working mom who will stop at nothing to be with her daughter, Donna is setting a wonderful example for Julana.

Julana and Donna at Donna's Graduation Ceremony

The Courtroom

> *"...Humor is an affirmation of dignity,*
> *a declaration of man's superiority to all that befalls him."*
>
> ~Romain Gary

The occasion was a somber one. I was accompanying 'SanSan,' one of my students into a windowless courtroom. On this day she had come to listen helplessly as the D.A. would officially charge her only son with First Degree Murder. The State said he shook his infant daughter to death. He was eighteen years old.

Other students had offered to join us - many had been in her shoes. I tried to act calm and poised as we maneuvered our way through the downtown courthouse plaza. This was the main hub for the local transit system and many of the city's homeless spent their days there sleeping on benches, playing cards or panhandling. As we made our way past the throngs of displaced and misplaced souls milling aimlessly about, the moment felt surreal. My students and I knew a lot of these people, and when asked where we were headed, a few eagerly joined our entourage either out of sincere concern or simply for lack of anything better to do. I felt like the Pied Piper - except I wasn't skipping.

Larry, SanSan's boy was also one of my students and I had good reason to believe he was innocent.

On the opposite side of the plaza, 'BabyGirl' had just gotten off the city bus.
She was coming from the Winn Dixie and was on her way home when she spotted us. "Hey, y'all, where you be goin'?" she yelled halfway across town.

SanSan and BabyGirl went back a long way. Both had seen more in their short lives than most of us could ever imagine. They were lucky to be alive and they knew it.

BabyGirl knew this was a tough one for her friend. "You know I'm witcha, girl," she declared in solidarity, and secured her place in the troupe. So looking like a funeral procession, we trudged into the dark, smelly lobby of the courthouse where we all knew the routine: "Place your possessions on the conveyor belt and proceed through the metal detector." Most of my "associates" had been in the bowels of this building more times than they wanted to remember, so they knew to travel light and to mind their own business. I was nearly in the elevator when the kind voice of a Security Guard pierced my numbness with an innocent question. "Excuse me, Miss, do these belong to you?"

As I returned to view the TV screen that would reveal my alleged belongings, I watched in horror at an X-ray image of what looked like the *claws* of some prehistoric creature floating nonchalantly past the camera. There, amidst the gauntlet of purses and cell phones that had been carefully placed on the courthouse conveyor belt, I suddenly became speechless. "Uh, no sir," I said stuttering, "I don't even know what that is!"

"Hey! 'Dem is *my* chicken feets!" BabyGirl yelled in a tone fraught with desperation and agitation. "Why is you tryin'

247

to give my chicken feets to her?"she demanded, glaring at the Security Officer.

"Well, ma'am, she was the last one through and I just thought…"

"Well, dat's your problem, you think too much! 'Dey is *my* chicken feets. Now hand 'dem over!"

By this time, we were all in hysterics. As I mentioned, BabyGirl had just come from the Winn Dixie, but she wasn't about to miss out on an opportunity to get the firsthand scoop by worrying about perishable items! She frantically stuffed her provisions into the plastic bag from which they had escaped, and hurried onto the elevator. On our way up, we were still chuckling and SanSan couldn't help herself. She curled her fingers into the shape of a claw and pretended to peck at me like a giant deranged chicken. *"Beware the Claw!"* she grinned and cackled like the wicked witch. I shook my head, rolled my eyes and laughed out loud. SanSan has a tough exterior but she's incredibly witty and in light of the situation at hand, we all needed a good laugh.

As we reached the third floor and found the right room, we took our seats amongst a sea of expressionless faces. The courtroom was packed with family members hoping to steal a glance of their loved one as they stood before the judge. Although our purpose there was solemn, I was still smirking as I thought about *'the claw.'* Then without warning, Larry was escorted into the room in shackles and handcuffs and we were all reminded of the severity of the moment. *"State of Florida vs. Larry Smith,"* the bailiff shouted. He was over six feet tall and lanky with an air of innocence about him. He stood there helpless and despondent, and he hung his head as the judge approached the bench. He looked back at us and attempted to smile. I felt tears welling up and the sudden onset of helplessness overcame me.

As the judge silently reviewed the file, a seriously disheveled homeless man entered the courtroom and quickly spotted the only empty seat. Unfortunately, it was at the end of *our* row. We all stood and did our best to accommodate him as he politely excused himself and side-stepped his way to the vacant spot in the courtroom pew. But as fate would have it, he accidentally stepped on someone's foot - the *wrong* foot. Before he could get the second syllable of "Sor-ry" out of his mouth, SanSan hauled off and slugged him hard, right in the leg and yelled, "What is you *crazy?* You stepped on my damn foot!"

"I'm so sorry, ma'am," the man pleaded in vain.

"Sorry?! Damn straight you *is* sorry, now get off my foot - shit!"

"Is there a problem?" the judge asked impatiently.

"No sir," I said, and shot a glance at SanSan. Emotion had gotten the best of her, and without thinking, she ignored the judge and looked right at me, "Yes dey is a problem! He stepped on my damn foot, and he stink! I don't care what you say, he ain't sittin' next to me!"

Nervous laughter filled the room, and even though I sensed a slight hint of amusement in his expression, the judge had dozens of more cases as serious as this one to hear that day, and he was losing patience. He read the charge out loud, and then looked at Larry for the first time. "How do you plead, young man?"

"Not guilty Your Honor," he said in a low, shaky voice as he looked to the floor. With a loud bang, the gavel hit its mark and we all jumped in our seats. The show was over and Larry was escorted out of the room. He never looked back. He would be sentenced to fifteen years in prison for a crime many of us believed he did not commit.

As an educator teaching in the most daunting of circumstances, I have discovered and embraced the delicate balance between humor and despair. When faced with darkness, absurdity is often as welcome as a long lost friend - and somewhere buried in the space between madness and sanity, lies downright salvation.

So here's to you, SanSan and BabyGirl. Thank you for giving us the gift of laughter in the face of hopelessness. I will never forget you.

> *"...A simple child, that lightly draws its breath and feels its life in every limb,*
> *what should it know of death?"*
>
> ~William Wordsworth

She looked like an angel in her sweet little white starched dress – the one with a small, delicate pink rose embroidered on the front. It had short, puffy sleeves and was trimmed with lace. Her mom bought it for her at WalMart for the occasion. She was so tiny and beautiful; her dark skin smooth and flawless; her hair soft and curly. She was just six weeks old and she was everything her family had ever dreamed of.

I remember looking at her lying there so peaceful and still. I remember how it touched my very soul that I had never known the sheer joy of giving birth. I remember shaking and sobbing silently as I gently stroked her hair and held her tiny little hand in mine. She didn't cry when her mother lifted up her dress to show me the scar. She couldn't. Because on this day, just 72 hours after the autopsy, she was in God's house, and her

18-year-old father was in jail charged with First Degree Murder.

The police report said he shook his infant daughter to death. The medical report said that her tiny brain had disintegrated from smashing against the inside of her skull. Born a victim of the relentless poverty that is choking the life out of our society, she didn't have a chance. Her dad, Larry, was one of my GED students at the county jail. When we met, he had been locked up for stealing diapers for his 2-year-old son because at sixteen and without a high school diploma, he couldn't get a job. This boy was kind and gentle and respectful, and I believed he was innocent.

During the weeks that would follow, I felt shamefully inadequate. I knew that a person was innocent until proven guilty and I was driven to do what I could to help this kid. I was a teacher, a respected member of the community, a Guardian *Ad Litem*. And I was white. Surely they'd listen to me, right?

Even though I called the lead detective and told him I had information that could possibly change the course of this young man's life, he was unresponsive. Even though I told him that I knew people who would corroborate my declaration, he said it was a "non-issue." Even though we were told that the baby had been dropped on the floor just hours after arriving home from the hospital, he became agitated and said "listen, lady, I don't care if someone played basketball with that baby; it's a non-issue."

So here's to you, detective: I'm sure you were a fair cop at some point in your career. I'm sure you tried to do your best to give people the benefit of the doubt and to defend the Constitutional rights of every human being. I'm sure you even used to see them as *human beings.* We live and hope.

A little more than a year later, Larry was transferred to a maximum-security prison. He would be surrounded by grown men – some savages – with nothing to lose. *Evil exposes itself in many forms.*

In the beginning, he would call me collect every night, some nights two and three times, because as long as he was on the phone, the other inmates, many of them animals, would leave him alone. My heart ached every time the phone rang. I couldn't stand the thought of the sheer horror he must have been experiencing. I had this image of him in my head: a tall, lanky, insecure kid trying to stroll casually toward the phones because some sadistic inmate was trying to best him.

I want you to know Larry's story. I want you to understand the plight of those who were born into extreme poverty. I want you to walk a mile in his shoes. I want you to forgive yourself for judging people before you truly understand their circumstances. I want you to thank God for *everything* you have.

The morning Larry called 911, he did so because his infant daughter, who had been left in his care for the umpteenth time since her birth, began spitting up and suddenly became unconscious. He was frantic when he ran to his neighbor's apartment to use her phone. His girlfriend had their cell phone and she had, once again made up an excuse to leave Larry, the baby and their two year old son alone in the apartment. She claimed to be looking for a job. The neighbors thought it was odd that she was rarely home to care for her newborn baby. They gossiped amongst themselves and speculated as to why she would leave for hours at a time, sometimes an entire day. They felt sorry for Larry who was just a boy himself.

Prior to the 911 call, Larry had gone to the neighbor's on at least two occasions. He asked the women if it was normal that the baby had been sleeping for nearly fourteen hours straight. He wondered if he should wake her up to feed her. He even asked if he should call an ambulance. The neighbors shared with me how strange it was that the baby was so lethargic all the time. They said it just wasn't normal that she would sleep so much. Larry's girlfriend told him not to pay any attention to them. She told them to mind their business. She said she and Larry were lucky to have such a good baby.

After the EMT's arrived, Larry accompanied the baby to the hospital. His mother, his sisters and I met him there. His girlfriend walked nonchalantly into the ER, shook her head, looked Larry dead in the eyes and said: "Larry, what have you done?"

He was in shock, but coherent enough to know that her question was absurd. Later that night, a detective came knocking. As he began firing questions, mainly at Larry, he told him that he was not being investigated, but that he simply wanted to know what had happened. He did not read Larry his Miranda Rights. Larry spoke honestly and from his heart. He told the detective he was in the kitchen warming a bottle of milk and when he went to feed the baby, she was lying on the bed crying. He bounced her on his knee, just like his girlfriend showed him how to do. Then all of a sudden, she began to spit up, her eyes rolled into the back of her head, and the crying stopped. The detective thanked him, gave Larry his card and told him to call if he remembered anything else.

The next morning, Larry did call with something he thought may be helpful. He remembered that his two year old son had been jumping up and down on the bed next to the sleeping infant. "Could that have jumbled things up in her head?" Larry asked innocently. As the detective took notes, he thanked Larry and commended him for being so cooperative and for doing his part to get to the bottom of things. As he scribbled the details on his tablet, he wrote in his report and testified in court that Larry had *"changed his story…"*

I ask you this: *Will you be prepared when they come knocking on your door or appear in the Emergency Room during your worst nightmare?* Ladies and Gentlemen, what will it take for us to stop judging one another and acknowledge that any parent could wake up to this kind of nightmare at any given moment? Has your child ever been involved in an innocent accident at home? A few bruises, maybe a cut? Did you know that marks of any kind on your child's body could constitute abuse? Maybe you were just horsing around, being a fun mom or dad, but things got a little crazy and someone got hurt.

Did you know that in the blink of an eye you could lose your children to a foster care system gone awry and face charges for an honest-to-goodness accident? You could go to jail if there was any question whatsoever that you meant to harm your own child. Sleep on that thought tonight, folks. *Sweet Dreams*.

Believe me, it is not my intention to minimize the severity of Larry's case, or to compare the horror of Shaken Infant Death Syndrome to a little family fun. I simply want you to understand the vulnerabilities in our laws and the split second in which a mishap could occur. Ever leave your child playing in the living room for just a moment and in the blink of an eye they're at the edge of the pool?

As an educator in a muddled system, I strive to protect the rights of innocent children and adults. I am one of countless citizens who are repulsed by abuse in any form. I am

260

however, one who believes from the depths of my soul that we also have a responsibility to stand up and fight for those who cannot defend themselves. I do my best to live by example and I do what I can to affect change.

Larry is halfway through his fifteen year sentence. He could sure use your prayers.

Larry and his Mom SanSan

Postscript

"The most I ever did for you was to outlive you, and that is much..."

~Edna St. Vincent Millay

It's been 21 years since my mother's untimely death.

She was my role model and my best friend. I am a teacher because of her.

It was the spring of 1991 when my dad, my brother and I gathered around her hospital bed and waited for the news we knew was coming but none of us wanted to hear. She had been in and out of the hospital for nearly eight months, enduring test after test and gradually getting worse. After about sixth months, Connie began to lose her balance and slur her words. We were helpless. My mother, my role model, my best friend, was slipping away. Like a thief in the night, late-stage brain cancer was rapidly stealing her individuality and robbing us of her remarkable spirit.

Paralyzed by the news of her illness, the remarkable people of Owego, New York confirmed their love and gratitude for my mother's unselfish efforts by blessing our family with phone calls, cards, flowers, casseroles and countless hours of heartfelt support. My sincere thanks and God bless you all.

After caring for her at home for as long as we could, we made the dreadful decision to put her in the care of professionals and admit her into the hospital. My dad, Leo, my brother Stephen and I spent our nights there and would go home in shifts. We would take a five minute shower, choke down something to eat, feed and walk the dogs and return to her side as soon as we could. On Easter Sunday of 1991, when I arrived alone at the hospital, the nurse's tentative approach made me suspicious. I felt my knees begin to buckle as they reluctantly and sympathetically informed me that Connie had "slipped peacefully into a coma."

For the first time during the roller coaster ride that was her brief illness, I was without my support network. No family, no friends, just me. Consumed by the shock of the moment, I was terrified, and like a little kid lost in the mall, I wanted my mom. My limbs were useless as I tried to make it from the nurse's station to my mother's bed. It was like running in slow motion, running from someone or something and unable to wake from a dark dream. When I conquered those final steps and came face-to-face with the reality of the situation, I simply could not accept the fact that she had left without saying goodbye.

Fighting back tears of pain and rage, I took her hand in mine, stroked her hair, kissed her on the cheek and said, *"I love you, Mom."* As they struggled with their own emotions, the nurses tried tenderly to explain that she may hear me but she could not respond. What they did not know, however, was that for as long as I can remember, my mom had established one steadfast rule in our house, one that was strictly enforced and on which she would not budge. According to "Connie-Law," no one in our family would go to bed angry, and we would never, *ever* leave the house without saying "I love you."

The tears burned in my eyes like acrid smoke, my throat closed up and I could barely breathe. The room was spinning and I was dizzy and nauseous. Through their own tears, the nurses tried to gently coax me out of the room. Then suddenly and to everyone's amazement, as I held tight to her listless hand, my mom sat up in bed, looked long into my eyes, hugged me hard and said, *"I love you, too."* So strong were her conviction and love for her family, that for a split second, Connie Lawrence defied the laws of the universe.

Those of us who knew her expected nothing less.

She closed those beautiful sky-blue eyes for the last time on that day and never opened them again. My mother died nine days later on April 9, 1991. She was 58.

Later that night, while sitting on my bed surrounded by my four best friends Jill, Brenda, Phyllis and Lynney, the

Cosmos erupted. Without warning, a severe and inexplicable electrical storm blew in and lasted nearly an hour.

It did not rain.

It did not snow.

It did not hail.

As we sat motionless, thunder and lightning held captive the night. With cracks and bangs and radiant streaks of unbridled energy, the pitch black April sky surrendered to the light, and through the deafening clamor of the thunder's wrath, God spoke.

When it was over, we sat there in silence and held on to each other tight. We held on to what was left of the truth. These girls loved my mom nearly as much as I did, and nothing needed to be said. Just as she had lived her life, Connie went out with a bang and was welcomed at her next stop with open arms.

....

The following week, hundreds of people flocked to Owego from all over the country with no more than a couple of days' notice just to pay their respects to a woman who had touched their hearts and changed their lives as their sixth grade teacher or elementary school principal. Our family endured a nine-hour wake as more than a thousand people waited in line for hours on a cold and rainy April day just to see her one more time.

The funeral itself was amazing. It had to be held in the local Baptist Church because there wasn't a funeral parlor in town that had the seating capacity required for a tribute of this magnitude. More than 500 people crammed into the pews and into folding chairs in the aisles, while another 300 or so gathered outside to listen on large speakers because there simply was no more room.

Our pastor, the Reverend Kenneth H. Simpson – a beacon in my mom's life – delivered a beautiful, powerful and fitting memorial. Afterward, he stepped from the altar and invited anyone who wanted to share stories about my mother to come up to the podium. Rev. Simpson was perhaps one of the few human beings (other than my mom) that I had ever met who actually practiced what he preached. His kind heart and tireless efforts have made this world a better place. God bless you, Ken.

Throughout the next couple of hours, friends, relatives, colleagues, students and local leaders fondly recalled Connie's pure heart, her electric smile, her hilarious poems, and her selfless dedication to the children and families of Tioga County.

For reasons I could not have fathomed then, I remember looking out into the vast sea of distraught and grieving faces and making eye contact with Juanita Heath. She was pleasant and honest and proud. She was a hard-working woman who often held down two or three jobs at any given time just to make ends meet for her kids' sake. She smiled sadly and sweetly and acknowledged my pain with a simple nod. Many people made that long walk to the altar that misty April morning, and the beautiful memories they shared to some extent pierced the armor of my numbness. But in the end, it was all blur to me, as if I were in a strange body watching the events unfold in front of me. Although I appreciated the courageous efforts of every single person who spoke of my mother's remarkable legacy, to this day, I remember little more than the agony I felt knowing we were there to say goodbye.

Then, Juanita Heath, the last to speak, took to the podium. In front of community leaders, administrators, educators, local merchants and God, she humbly looked into our eyes and said, "If it weren't for Connie Lawrence, there were many times when we wouldn't have had food on our table at Thanksgiving or toys under the tree at Christmas. I'm so sorry that I'll never be able to thank her properly again, but I'll never forget all she did for me and my kids. We loved her very much."

Such simple words from such a humble woman brought 800 people to their knees. *Yes, it takes a village.*

Wherever you are, Juanita, thank you and may God bless you.

My brother Stephen did the closing eulogy and again, I don't remember much, but I do remember being so proud of him. I also wondered how he was even standing, much less *speaking,* of our beloved mother. If I live to be 100, I'll never forget his final sentence. While holding back the floodgates of his own emotions, he said (remember this was in 1991), "So folks, if George Bush can get three standing ovations for one lame speech, I think Connie deserves at least one."

Slowly and with reverence, the crowd rose in unison. Then came the applause - people stood and clapped so loudly and with such purpose, I remember thinking that the stained glass windows would shatter all around us. People just kept standing and clapping and crying for what seemed like an eternity. No one wanted to sit down because we all knew that it would be over and that it would mean that she was really gone. Almost ten minutes later, I think people were actually in pain, but all were still standing and applauding, because stopping meant that we had to leave and gather at Connie's final resting place – a reality no one wanted to face.

As a result of that incredible event that was her funeral, I've come to believe that we, those of us sharing this earth, must strive to *do what we can* each and every day. We must stop judging and start caring. We must realize that ignorance breeds hatred and that indifference breeds disaster. I believe that if we simply remind ourselves that our time on this earth is precious and brief, perhaps we would commit more random acts of kindness. Perhaps we would love more and criticize less.

Finally, I believe that if we all lived as though one day someone like Juanita Heath might stand before God and speak with so much love at *our* funeral, that perhaps the daily dance to succeed would become much less significant, and we would know that true greatness lies in the most humble of actions.

Thank you for sticking with me on this long and often difficult journey.

Please remember how much you have to offer and how significant you are on this earth.

Please know how much you are loved and that we are all connected.

Please know that I value you and that I'll see you soon…

Speak your truth and do what you can.

Cheers…

Closing Thoughts...

> *"What lies behind us and what lies before us*
> *are small matters compared to what lies within us..."*
>
> ~Ralph Waldo Emerson

Catastrophic occurrences such as 9/11 and Hurricane Katrina reveal the tenacity and the depth of the human spirit. Every day calamities such as oppression, poverty, domestic violence, and extremism reveal the truth. I believe this may be the greatest tragedy of all.

The truth is that we, as a nation, are fast losing sight of that which has defined us for generations, and because we are relentlessly bombarded by the 'spin' of the times, our core values are being put to the test. The United States has become a battlefield on which Americans are pitted against Americans: Red/Blue, Liberal/ Conservative, Christian/Non-Christian, Pro Life/Pro Choice, the list goes on and on and we all pay the price. I believe people are basically decent and kind, and we *are* capable of creating change. Our ability to dig in and help our fellow man is evident in the most challenging of times, but the call to greatness must be trumpeted from every town square – today, before apathy becomes the standard. We must plunge into the darkest places of our history and remind ourselves how we got here and how many died fighting for our right to be free. We must speak to our children about the sacrifices made by combat veterans and by crusaders like Nelson Mandela, Alice Paul, Medgar Evers, Eleanor Roosevelt, Yitzhak Rabin, Mamie Till, and countless others who envisioned a better future and acted. We must remember those who acted because their cause was in the best interest of every man, woman and child, not because it served their own purpose; and those who acted and often risked their lives to secure basic human rights for all, not just for a privileged few.

I believe in authenticity and individuality and in the right of every human being to feel safe and honored and respected for who they are and for the life they choose to lead.

I believe in the enormity of suffering. I witness it in many forms as a GED teacher and a Guardian Ad Litem in a southern college town that struggles to deal with the bane of cultural discourse. Together with my colleagues, we battle every day to convince many of our students that an honest days' work and a high school diploma far outweigh the lure of easy money and the badges associated with it. It is an uphill climb, but we keep trying. We keep trying because we believe it is both our gift as well as our duty.

I believe it starts with each and every one of us who are unwilling to tolerate the disparity that separates the haves from the have-nots. It starts when we leave the comfort of our home every morning and make a decision to do something, *any*thing that will affect change.

The time has come to wake up, stand up, step up and speak up. I believe that most people truly want to do the right thing, yet may not always know what that is. Here are a few suggestions to jumpstart a movement: perhaps you'll consider donating some of your *good* clothes, not the old and outdated ones, to a shelter for battered women. You'd be surprised how little it takes to help boost someone's self esteem, especially when they're interviewing for their first job in years. Perhaps you'll acknowledge that your kids don't need another video game, an upgraded cell phone or a plasma TV, and maybe you'll donate that money to the Red Cross or a local charity. Perhaps, instead of another trip to the mall, you and your family will volunteer at a homeless shelter - these people are human beings like you and me, and whether any of us want to admit it, ***hard times are just a layoff away.***

I believe in humanity and I believe in humility. I believe we must do what we can.

> "Come to the edge - we can't, we're afraid.
> Come to the edge – we can't, we'll fall.
> Come to the edge – and they did – and he pushed them –
> and they flew…"
>
> *~Apollinaire*

From the beginning of this project, I promised myself I would do my best not to leave you feeling helpless or hopeless. The content of some of my stories is extreme, and most don't have happy endings, but that's life, isn't it?... Not always.

I believe in the power of the human spirit and in our unique ability to transform ourselves. Oscar Wilde once wrote, "We *are all in the gutter but some of us are looking up at the stars."* Whether you believe it or not, you have a great deal to offer.

While searching for more ways to motivate and inspire my students, I sat down one day and composed a letter. It took less than five minutes to write because I believed so strongly in its message. I personalize each one and present it to each student in silence the week before they take their GED exam. Grown men and women cry openly and hug me without shame.

My juveniles fidget and wipe away tears they want no one else to see them shed. They usually "half-hug" me on their way out the door, the way they would hug their home boy in public. But I know how moved they really are.

I must preface the closing words of my letter: 'Go To Your Destiny,' by giving credit where credit is due. On her show one afternoon during the Olympic Games in Atlanta, Oprah Winfrey interviewed twin brothers, both distance runners and strong contenders from Africa. These men had been running their entire lives and before the start of every race, they would hug each other and say, "Go To Your Destiny." I use this phrase all the time. Thank you, Oprah, for discovering the authenticity in those remarkable men and for sharing them with those of us who also do our best to enlighten and empower others on a daily basis.

You Are Here...

Dear Donna,

What you are about to do requires an incredible amount of courage.

- You are here because you've worked extremely hard.
- You are here because you have the intelligence, the skill and the determination it takes to succeed.
- You are here because you want something so badly that you've made the tough decision to do whatever it takes to get it.
- You are here because you've earned the right to be.
- You are here because you about to change the course of your destiny.
- You are here because behind bars is *not* where you are meant to be.

- You are here because you were not born to simply exist – you were born to *soar*.

- You are here because your time has come…

The day you take your GED exam will be a day that you will remember for the rest of your life. Know what you know, stay focused, and keep your eye on the ball. It will be a long day, but when it's over, you will have done something extraordinary for you and for your family.

Please know that I am incredibly proud of you.

To you, Donna Arnold, I say welcome to your future and congratulations!

Go To Your Destiny …

Leanne

> *"No one can make you feel inferior without your consent…"*
> ~Eleanor Roosevelt

Muddled hopelessly in the debate between Liberal and Conservative, Pro-Choice and Pro-Life, Gay Marriage and One Man/One Woman, School Prayer and Separation of Church and State, I see a lost opportunity. In my fellow Americans, I see discord and disconnect. It's as if we've lost sight of that which keeps us grounded and whole. I believe we've become so rabid and competitive, we've forgotten that *simplicity, silence, gratitude, and gra*ce are necessary components of our daily existence. Since Eleanor Roosevelt is one of the most influential historical figures in my life, I'll share with you, as I do with my students, a daily reflection that if heeded, could change the world…

While teaching part time at The Todhunter School for Girls in New York State, Mrs. Roosevelt teamed with the school's founders and provided their students with the following meditation. Each girl was required to memorize these words and recite them each morning. I find the secret to world peace in its message. It has become part of my daily meditation and I share it every chance I get.

"O, God –

Give us clean hands, clean words, and clean thoughts.
Help us to stand for the hard right against the easy wrong.
Teach us to work as hard and play as fair, in Thy sight alone,
as though all the world was watching.
Keep us ready to help others and send us chances every day
to do a little good, and so grow more like Christ.
Amen"

If 'God' and 'Christ' are not your driving forces, don't judge or make excuses - fill in the blanks.

Peace...

> *"Let us not be satisfied with just giving money. Money is not enough, money can be got, but they need your hearts to love them. So, spread your love everywhere you go…"*
>
> ~Mother Teresa

As you segue into the final phase of this project, I feel compelled to share the following anecdote with you. It sure empowered me…

I believe Millard and Linda Fuller are two of the most important people of our time, and I'll bet you don't even recognize their names, do you? They are the founders of Habitat for Humanity. While listening to NPR a couple of years ago, I heard an enchanting interview with Mr. Fuller as he recounted his anxiety over an upcoming speaking engagement at Harvard University. The interview went something like this:

Mr. Fuller told the interviewer that he had often visited recipients of Habitat homes. During one such visit, he sat in the home of an elderly African American woman and shared with her how nervous he was over a pending speech he had been asked to give. She was in her 80's and had endured a great deal throughout her life. She had suffered many hardships, overcome many challenges and considered having her own home the highlight of all those years of struggle. The woman asked where he would be speaking and when he told her it was Harvard, she innocently wondered aloud why he was so nervous. He explained that this was Harvard University, an academic seat of our nation's future leaders, a group of brilliant young men and women who would be expecting to hear something extraordinary. He said he was fretful because he really didn't know what he was going to say to them.

"Well, you only gots to tell them one thing," she offered matter-of-factly. "Please enlighten me!" he pleaded. "All you gots to tell them is that if they wants to go up, they gots to know what it means to be down."

We should all strive to be so free.

APPENDIX

> *"It is the greatest of all mistakes to do nothing because you can only do a little..."*
>
> ~Sydney Smith

Amongst the following pages is an abundance of opportunity to enable you and empower you to *do what you can.* First and foremost, I have provided a list of **HOTLINES & IMPORTANT PHONE NUMBERS.** If you or someone you know requires the services of the capable and compassionate people who will answer your call, *please* pick up the phone. If you are reporting abuse, you can remain anonymous – but please don't allow the victim to remain invisible. You absolutely *must* do *what you can* as someone's life may depend on it. I have also included sections on volunteering and mentoring, as well as reputable and worthy contribution opportunities. Remember, the pen is mightier than the sword, so write your representative, write to your long-lost relative, or write a check – whatever inspires you.

Martin Luther King, Jr. once said, "Philanthropy is commendable, but it must not cause the philanthropist to overlook the circumstances of economic injustice which make philanthropy necessary."

There are also websites designed specifically for philanthropic purposes. If you decide that working in a homeless shelter or mentoring is not for you, visit one of these credible sites – the possibilities are limitless.

In my 20 or so years as an educator and student of the universe, I have become increasingly conscious of the value of a healthy paradigm shift. Remember, pain is relative, and although yours is no less or no greater than mine, when suffering is put in perspective, our innate desire to be helpful in some way trumps self-loathing. And that's a beautiful thing.

As the actor Robert Urich said after being diagnosed with cancer, "There comes a time in life when either you define the moment, or the moment defines you."

My friends, for all of its capacity and potential, the internet is locking us behind closed doors. Although we call them 'Social Networks,' we are becoming more hidden and less approachable. Please take the time to notice what websites your kids are frequenting and who they hang out with. Get out from behind your own computer and be aware of the activities of your family and friends. Please don't let them disappear.

Crisis Hotline Numbers

- **Rape Hotline:** **800.656.4673**
- **National Child Abuse Hotline:** **800.25ABUSE (800.252.2873)**
- **National Domestic Violence Hotline: 800.799.SAFE(7233)**
- **National Elder Abuse Hotline: 800.252.8966**
- **National Human Trafficking H.L.: 888.373.7888**
- **Crisis Intervention/Suicide Hotline: 800.448.3000/800.448.1833 (TDD)**
- **Bullying Hotline 855. 979.HELP (4357)**
- **Missing/Exploited Children Hotline: 800.235.3535**

- **Runaway Hotline**   **800.621.4000**

  (to report a runaway)

- **Confidential Runaway Hotline**   **800.231.6946**

  (for runaways)

- **Dating Abuse Helpline**   **866.331.9474**

  (loveisrespect.com)

- **Drug/Alcohol Abuse:**   **800.521.7128**

- **Dog Fighting Hotline:**   **877.847.4787**

<u>Charitable Giving Websites</u>:

- **jumo.com**
- **globalgiving.org**
- **give.org**
- **donorschoose.org**

Please don't forget about the needs right in your own community. Become a mentor, a Big Brother/Big Sister, or a Guardian *Ad Litem*. There are young people out there waiting for you. I strongly encourage you to visit your local nursing home or assisted living facility. Many of these folks are incredibly wise and funny and have so much to share.

Unfortunately, many of them sit there alone and depressed and longing for human contact. If you go, bring a tape recorder and ask some of these remarkable people to share their stories; your lives will be better for it. Go to the Big Brothers/Big Sisters website @ **bbbsa.org** or to **guardianadlitem.org**

Please visit your local animal shelter and cuddle abandon cats and walk homeless dogs. Even better, how about fostering or adopting a furry friend and prevent them from being euthanized? Many communities, including mine in central Florida, are blazing new trails toward the goal of true no-kill shelters.

Think before you acquire an animal. Don't support puppy mills; adopt a pet from a shelter or a rescue group, or open your home to the stray cat that keeps coming around and peeking in your window. These animals will bring so much joy to your family that you'll wonder who rescued whom! Teach your children the value of kindness and humanity toward animals – even the strays. Gandhi once said, "The greatness of a nation and its moral progress can be judged by the way its animals are treated."

Help your kids or someone else's prepare for a wonderful experience. You can absolutely make this world a better place by simply sharing your home, your skills, your time and yourself. Whatever you choose, you'll have done something incredible – Congratulations!

Go to *Your* Destiny.

Citations

Maya Angelou (1928 -) Pulitzer Prize winning American Poet/Author

Guillaume Apollinaire (1880 – 1918) French Poet and Critic

Francis Bacon (1561 – 1626) British Statesman/Philosopher

W.E.B. Dubois (1868 – 1963) American Author, Historian, Civil Rights Activist

Ralph Waldo Emerson (1803 – 1882) American Essayist/Poet

Erasmus (1466 – 1526) Humanist/Scholar

F. Scott Fitzgerald (1896 – 1940) American Author

Anne Frank (1929 – 1945) German-born Author: *Diary of a Young Girl*; Holocaust victim

Romain Gary (1914 – 1980) French Novelist/Diplomat

Maxim Gorky (1868 – 1936) Russian Dramatist/Novelist

The Haggadah Jewish text that sets forth the order of the Passover Seder

Don Henley (1947 -) /American Singer/Songwriter

Franz Kafka (1883 – 1924) Prague-born German Language Author

Toyohiko Kagawa (1888 – 1960) Japanese Evangelist, Pacifist, Social Advocate

John F. Kennedy (1917 – 1963) American President

Dalai Lama (1935 –) Exiled Spiritual Leader of Tibet, Nobel Prize Winner for Peace

Walter Lippman (1889 – 1974) American Writer, Reporter

Audre Lord (1934 – 1992) Caribbean-American Writer, Poet, Activist

Nelson Mandela (1918 –) Former South African President; Anti-Apartheid Activist

Alan Paton (1903 – 1988) South African author and Anti-Apartheid Activist

Edna St. Vincent Millay (1892 – 1950) Pulitzer Prize winning American Poet

Mother Teresa (1910 – 1997) Nobel Prize winning founder of Missionaries of Charity

Fredrich Nietzsche (1844 – 1900) German Philosopher, Poet

Casare Pavese (1908 – 1950) Italian Poet, Novelist and Translator

Eleanor Roosevelt (1884 – 1962) First Lady, Humanitarian, Writer, Advocate

Albert Schweitzer (1875 – 1965) German Theologian, Philosopher, Humanitarian

Sydney Smith (1764 – 1840) English Writer, Clergyman

Shania Twain (1965 -) Canadian-born Singer/Songwriter

Oscar Wilde (1854 – 1900) Irish Writer/Poet

Oprah Winfrey (1954 -) American Media Mogul, Actress, Author, Philanthropist

William Wordsworth (1770 – 1850) English Romantic Poet